THE LABYRINTH:

A TRANSFORMING

RITUAL

Jonny Baker

THE LABYRINTH: A TRANSFORMING RITUAL

YTC Press
www.ytcpress.com
Monograph Series

YTC Press

An imprint dedicated to research on Youth, Theology & Culture

First published in 2007 by
YTC Press
– A Division of Youth Focus –
www.ytcpress.com
www.youthfocus.biz

ISBN: 978-1-84799-772-2

Copyright © 2007 Jonny Baker

All rights reserved. No part of this book may be reproduced or transmitted in any form or by any means, electronic or mechanical, including photocopying, recording, or by any information storage and retrieval system, without permission in writing from the publisher.

Youth Focus

Youth Focus is a partnership dedicated to providing good quality resources for those involved in Christian youth ministry at an affordable price. We undertake this ministry by

- Training volunteer, part-time and full-time youth workers throughout the world through our accredited online Emerge Academy, www.emergeacademy.net
- Providing lecture resources (scripts, handouts and PowerPoint presentations) for those involved in teaching youth ministry and associated disciplines, www.youthfocus.biz
- Publishing books, with our YTC Imprint through www.lulu.com, on youth ministry, ecclesiology, cultural studies, theology, education and associated disciplines

Youth Focus is based in the UK but partners with organisations around the world.

For more information, please contact Steve Griffiths through steve@youthfocus.biz or go to the websites:

www.youthfocus.biz
www.emergeacademy.net
www.ytcpress.com

This book is dedicated to
Kev, Ana and Brian who set me off on the labyrinth journey

Contents

	Acknowledgements	xi
Chapter One	Introduction	13
Chapter Two	The Labyrinth	17
Chapter Three	Ritual	27
Chapter Four	Making Sense of St. Paul's Labyrinth	45
Chapter Five	Concluding Remarks	83
Appendix One	Labyrinth Meditations	85
	Bibliography	99

Acknowledgments

Kev and Ana Draper first introduced me to the labyrinth when they installed their own version of it at Grace. A group of us then met to create what became the St Paul's Cathedral Labyrinth for the millennium. That group was myself, Ana Draper, Steve Collins, Ian Mobsby and Clara Swinson. Steve Collins came up with the design of the pathway and the rest of us helped create the content. Proost (www.proost.co.uk) came on board to help produce the meditation CD in a very short space of time. Lots of other people helped create aspects of the media at the various stations on the journey - notably Brian Draper, Jon Birch, Bruce Stanley, Mark Waddington, and OSBD.

The alternative worship movement as a whole has been the fertile ground in which this creative approach to worship has flourished. I owe them so much, not just in terms of this project but in terms of re-imagining how Christian faith can be fleshed out in culture.

The communities Grace, Moot (then Epicentre) and L8r helped install and staff the labyrinth. YFC then got behind the project to tour UK cathedrals.

Group Publishing had the vision to publish it as a resource for churches in the USA and Proost followed suit in the UK. Since then the labyrinth has become a global phenomenon translated into several languages.

Pete Ward was my supervisor at Kings College, London on the dissertation. He has been a friend and mentor to me in many ways.

Thanks to Steve Griffiths for the desire to see this published beyond just the university library bookshelf.

Introduction

In March 2000, a labyrinth was set up in St Paul's Cathedral, London for one week. Described on the advertising flyer as, 'an interactive installation for spiritual journeys', it consisted of a pathway mapped on the ground for the participants to follow. *En route*, there were various stations[1] at which the participant paused to listen to a track of music and a meditation on a Discman[2] and participate in some symbolic or ritual action. The labyrinth incorporated a mix of items recognizably within the tradition of Christian worship, things used in everyday life and current technology. It was designed and constructed by

---

[1] A station is a term current in alternative worship groups for a physical area where the worshipper stops and participates by observation, prayer or some ritual act such as lighting a candle. Its origins may well be in the practice of visiting Stations of the Cross at Easter in many church traditions

[2] Sony's personal stereo portable CD players were called Discmans. As with Sony's cassette Walkman, this has become the familiar term for all makes of portable CD players

various 'alternative worship'[3] groups in London as a special millennium celebration and outreach event. It was a somewhat surprising sight to see artifacts of popular culture in the context of St Paul's Cathedral - flickering television screens, CD players and computers. It was the kind of art installation that would seem to have been more at home across the new Millennium Bridge on the other side of the Thames in the Tate Modern rather than in a traditional cathedral setting of Christian worship. In spite of this, it was deemed to be a success[4] by most participants, the Cathedral staff and the organizers, many of whom found it a very powerful experience.

The St Paul's Labyrinth is described in further detail in Chapter Two following a brief overview of labyrinths and cathedral labyrinths in particular. Walking a labyrinth is a ritual act. To help make sense of what is happening when someone participates in it, the tools of ritual theory are used. In Chapter Three, following a brief discussion of approaches to ritual theory, newer studies are drawn upon, in particular the work of Catherine Bell.[5] Rather than focusing on the universal qualities of what makes something a ritual, she focuses on the ritualized act as a form of practice. The four features of human activity as practice she describes are that it

---

[3] Alternative worship is a term used to describe various Christian groups who are seeking to develop worship that engages with post modern culture. For a further discussion of the term and what the worship is like see Paul Roberts booklet *Alternative Worship in the Church of England* (Roberts, 1999, p3-9)
[4] Success is very difficult to quantify. It is here used to describe the overall impression given from the various parties mentioned. The detail of the success or otherwise for participants and planners is explored later in this book
[5] Bell, 1992

is situational; strategic; embedded in a misrecognition of what it is in fact doing and able to reconfigure a vision of the order of power in the world, or 'redemptive hegemony'.[6] Bell's framework is used to discuss and make sense of the St Paul's Labyrinth in Chapter Four. The 'postmodern times'[7] we live in are discussed in the section on practice as situational. Two trends - the rise of consumerism, and the development of new technologies – and their impact on faith and religion are explored. In the section on practice as strategic, alternative worship will be discussed as a strategy for relating to the institutional church and contemporary culture. The trickster character of mythology and Turner's notion of liminality[8] are used in considering how ritual is strategically used to negotiate change within a tradition. The final strategy considered is the language employed to talk about God. Bell's notion of misrecognition is contested as patronizing. How individual participants are transformed, becoming ritualized agents endowed with a sense of ritual mastery with which to live in the real world will be discussed too. The process of participants' negotiation of meaning via consent and resistance is the final consideration. The Concluding Remarks posit that the St Paul's Labyrinth offers a clue to the potential strategic use of religion and ritual as a cultural resource for negotiation and resistance, for mapping meaning routes through the postmodern maze, for empowering individuals to be ritualized agents who are both culturally engaged and resistant at the same time, who are both postmodern and Christian.

---

[6] Bell, 1992, p.81
[7] The phrase 'postmodern times' is taken from David Lyon (Lyon, 2000)
[8] Turner, 1969

I was involved in the process of developing and running the St Paul's Labyrinth as a member of the core planning group. In this respect the perspective offered is as an insider rather than an outsider, emic rather than etic criticism.[9] There are plusses and minuses in any research situation.[10] In hindsight, the tools of analysis are often shown to conform to whatever subtle purposes the larger analysis serves.[11] It is now widely recognized that neutrality and objectivity were a fiction at the best of times.[12] So the perspective here is self-consciously an embedded one from an interested participant rather than a detached observer. It is offered here with humility as part of an ongoing discussion about culture, ritual and religion in postmodern times.

---

[9] Grimes, 1990, p.19
[10] Glazier, 1997, p.7
[11] Bell, 1992, p.14
[12] Brueggemann, 1993, p.6-12

The Labyrinth

Mazes and a range of labyrinth designs are found all round the world in various cultures and civilizations. They are found carved in rock, ceramics, clay tablets, mosaics, manuscripts, stone patterns, turf, hedges, and cathedral pavements. They are well documented by Jeff Saward.[1] He is recognized to be the leading authority in the world today on labyrinths according to The Labyrinth Society.[2] The earliest known designs are about 3000 years old. The most famous one from ancient times was the Cretan one, the lair of the mythological Minotaur, which Theseus slew with the aid of Ariadne and her spool of thread.[3] Whilst there seems to be plenty of

---

[1] Saward, 1999
[2] The Labyrinth Society is an American organisation. Their web site is www.geomancy.org/tls
[3] De Freitas, 1987, p.411

information on designs found in various places around the world, the significance of them for the various cultures they were part of and the story of how they developed from one place to another (or simultaneously appeared in several) is much harder to fathom. The documentation is fairly scant. They are variously linked with being a site for the ritual re-enactment of ancient myths,[4] with pilgrimage,[5] with descent into the unconscious, Mother Earth, or Hades and subsequent ascent to the Sacred Mountain,[6] as a ritual of protection from evil spirits,[7] with playing games and dancing,[8] being decorative, and in more recent times as a spiritual tool for personal transformation.[9] Saward describes their usage, development and the mythologies associated with them as 'complex and difficult to trace'[10] and Deedes concludes his essay by saying 'however many clues we may yet discover, it is doubtful whether we shall ever know its mystery'.[11]

Cathedral Labyrinths

Labyrinths were a feature of many medieval cathedrals.[12] One of the best remaining examples is found in Chartres Cathedral in Northern France. In recent times, pilgrims have taken to traveling to

---

[4] Deedes, 1935, p.22-30
[5] Corbett, 1998
[6] De Freitas, 1987, p.413-414
[7] Saward, 1999, p.19
[8] De Freitas, 1987, p.414
[9] Artress, 1995, p.20-21
[10] Saward, 1999, p.2
[11] Deedes, 1935, p.42
[12] A list of church labyrinths in Europe is to be found on page 14 of *Ancient Labyrinths of the World* (Saward, 1999). The majority are found in Northern France.

Chartres specifically to walk the labyrinth. This kind of labyrinth is marked out on the floor, constructed in either coloured stone or tiles and usually between 10 and 40 feet in diameter.[13]

A common misconception is that a labyrinth is a maze. But unlike a maze, a labyrinth is unicursal. It has one well-defined path that weaves its way to the centre and back out again. There is only one entrance and exit, no dead ends, and no crossing of paths with a choice of which way to turn.[14] There is a range of designs in the various cathedrals.[15] Without doubt, the Chartres labyrinth is a stunning piece of design.

Several pieces of literature expound the 'sacred geometry' incorporated in the design.[16] Sacred Geometry focused on architectural design that created a serene and balanced climate for the human soul, an abode of eternal truth.[17] Lauren Artress devotes several pages to describing how the design was constructed.[18] She seems particularly fixated on the intricacies of the design as being

---

[13] Saward, 1999, p.12

[14] The unicursal nature of the labyrinth applies to all the cathedral type of labyrinths. However the distinction is less clear in ancient labyrinths. It was clearly possible to get lost in the Cretan labyrinth as Theseus found his way out again by following the ball of thread. In other popular uses, the term labyrinth is also used to describe something more akin to a maze.

[15] Helmut Kern's book *Labyrinthe* is the most comprehensive book available on labyrinths. It incorporates several photographs of cathedral labyrinths. For simpler diagrams of the various main designs see Saward, 1999 p.10-17

[16] See, for example, *Sacred Geometry, Philosophy and Practice* by Robert Lawlor, 1982. Following the links from the Caerdroia web site also reveals a current fascination with sacred geometry – see www.ilc.tsms.soton.ac.uk/caerdroia

[17] Lawlor, 1982, p.10

[18] Artress, 1995, p.55-67

one of the keys to what makes the labyrinth so successful. On the Chartres labyrinth, there are lunations around the edge. Artress describes walking onto a labyrinth replica without the lunations as being like 'walking into a tin can with no resounding energy' and says that 'without them the power of the labyrinth is reduced'.[19]

Surprisingly, it is very difficult to ascertain what purpose the labyrinth served in the life of the cathedrals in the Middle Ages. There are also contradictions in the literature that is available. Jean Favier states, 'Many medieval churches have a labyrinth in the nave floor, signifying pilgrimage towards Jerusalem in this world and the road to Salvation in the next world. A symbol of the Christian way, the labyrinth has never really been used for any religious practices'.[20] But another perspective states 'Labyrinths generally symbolized the path of the soul through life and medieval pilgrims re-enacted this, following the path of the labyrinth in the cathedral on their knees, symbolizing the journey to Jerusalem'.[21] Christians in the Middle Ages vowed to visit Jerusalem once in their life, but in the wake of the Crusades, seven cathedrals were appointed as substitutes by the Roman church. Artress suggests that the walk into the labyrinth marked the ritual end of the pilgrimage.[22] Other suggestions include people walking it on the eve of their baptism or confirmation,[23] as an aid to contemplative prayer in Holy Week,[24] and as an illustration both of the life of the Christian and of the life

---

[19] Artress, 1995, p.62
[20] Favier, 1988, p.26
[21] Cowan, 1979, p.98
[22] Artress, 1995, p.32
[23] Riddell, Pierson and Kirkpatrick, 2000, p.149
[24] Riddell, Pierson and Kirkpatrick, 2000, p.149

of Christ.[25]

The St Paul's Labyrinth

The St Paul's labyrinth is a contemporary version of a cathedral labyrinth that incorporates music, art, media and activities at intervals along the path. Several alternative worship groups in London – Grace, LOPE, and Epicentre – had met together to discuss and plan what would be a good way to celebrate the millennium. The idea of doing a labyrinth in St Paul's Cathedral was the result of that meeting. Following discussions and negotiations with staff at the cathedral, permission was granted to run the labyrinth for a week at the beginning of Lent 2000 in one of the transepts off the main cathedral dome. The groups had run labyrinths in their own services before based on the design at Chartres Cathedral and laid out by using tape on the floor.[26] The way these were run was to have ambient music playing out loud with occasional scriptures and meditation read out as people walked the path with some things to do and read en route. There are a limited number of people who can go on a labyrinth at any one time so around the labyrinth were several other stations for prayer, meditation and ritual acts while people were waiting to go on.

Running a labyrinth for a week at St Paul's Cathedral presented several challenges to this approach, which significantly

---

[25] Saward, 1999, p.13
[26] Kev and Anna Draper of LOPE first developed the approach. In conversation with me, Anna explained that they had seen mention of labyrinths on the alternative worship Internet discussion group. Following that they searched the Internet, found the Chartres design and made the rest up! Grace and Epicentre picked up the approach inspired by LOPE

influenced the final version. The first challenge was the space in which the labyrinth was to be located. The Chartres design simply would not fit or work in that space. This was overcome by Steve Collins, an architect on the planning group, producing an original design to fit in the space of the transept in keeping with the square patterned tiles on the floor. This was made on a piece of cloth 11m x 11m and marked out with white gaffer tape. The second was that because of other activities in the Cathedral, music could not be played out loud. The music and readings were felt to be so important to the overall experience of walking the labyrinth that it was decided to use CD Discmans so that participants could listen on headphones. A CD of original music, readings and meditations was then produced for this. The third challenge was that the Cathedral staff didn't want stations around the labyrinth. This resulted in incorporating these into the labyrinth itself. These original features are (or at least were) unique to the St Paul's labyrinth. The final appearance was something akin to a contemporary art installation, self evidently constructed, playful, contemporary and interactive.

The guidebook that walkers were given describes the themes explored in the labyrinth as follows:

Journey – we are all journeying in our relationships. The labyrinth gives us the space to explore the highs and the lows of our journeys and to commit ourselves to journey onward.

Letting go – many of us live lives that are stressful and over-busy. The labyrinth is an opportunity to symbolically let go of the busyness that may spoil our relationships.

Centering – the journey around the labyrinth can symbolize a desire on our part to centre and focus our lives on God. At the centre we are free to meet God, sit and rest for a while.

Incarnation – in the original incarnation God came as Christ to share our experience of human existence. As we journey back out of the labyrinth, carrying something of our encounter with God, we are encouraged to be God's 'incarnation' in our own lives and world'.[27]

These closely parallel the three stages described by other contemporary groups using the labyrinth of purgation, illumination and union.[28] The stages had a practical outworking in the following ways:

1. Inward journey – listened to before entering the labyrinth to prepare the walker for the journey. Emphasizing themes of journey, relationship, letting go, centering, creation, the Trinity, Incarnation, and encounter with God, this paints a theological backdrop for the journey ahead.

2. Noise – images of an oscilloscope or sound line flicker on a stack of three televisions. The walker is encouraged to reflect on internal and external noise in her own life and to place it to one side, quiet down and listen for God's signal.

3. Letting go – the walker takes a stone from a pile, reflects on concerns, worries, pressures in his life and imagines letting go of them and offering them to God by dropping the stone into a pool of water.

4. Hurts – the walker draws symbols on a piece of paper to represent ways she has been hurt and ways she has hurt others. This is then screwed up and placed in the bin as a sign of confession,

---

[27] The Guidebook was produced specifically for the St Paul's labyrinth, and was translated into French, German, Spanish, Italian and Japanese as well as English. It can be obtained from www.labyrinth.org.uk

[28] See for example Corbett, 1998 and Artress, 1995, p.28

letting go and receiving forgiveness. Words of absolution conclude the meditation.

5. Distractions – a map, a compass and some magnets. The walker is encouraged to reflect on distractions 'false norths' that shift his focus away from God by moving the magnets near the compass and watching the needle being pulled away from true North. He then takes time to focus on God.

6. Holy Space – the walker has reached the centre of the labyrinth where there is space to sit down. There is a candle with three wicks burning to symbolize the Trinity and bread and wine is available. The walker takes time to be and to receive from God.

7. Outward journey – as the walker leaves the centre, this track prepares her for going back into the world, taking her encounter with God with her, and passing on what she has received.

8. Self – the walker looks into a mirror and listens to verses from Psalm 139 and contemplates being made in God's image, being loved by God. Her uniqueness is celebrated by placing a thumbprint in an open book.

9. Planet – a video of images of space and breathtaking waterfalls loops round as the walker is invited to contemplate their home, planet earth. He plants a seed in soil as a symbol of love and care for creation.

10 Others – a computer screen full of candles greets the walker and she is invited to think of the web of relationships within which she lives and pray for one or two others. This is symbolized by clicking on the candle with the computer mouse, which 'lights' the candle.

11 Impression – the walker leaves his footprints in sand and reflects on the impression or legacy he is leaving with his life.

12 Visitor's book – at the exit there is a visitor's book for the walker to record any comments or prayers.

To complete the labyrinth took approximately an hour, though clearly people could do it at their own pace. St Paul's Cathedral has a lot of tourists and pilgrims. The labyrinth was busy all week and walked by a whole range of people of different nationalities, the vast majority of whom had never encountered a labyrinth before – women, children, men, young, old, Christian, non-Christian, Jewish, Hindu, nuns, a bishop, and cathedral staff.

How do we make sense of the St Paul's labyrinth with its mix of ancient and postmodern, medieval pathways and current technology, and alternative worship located in the heart of institutional religion? The response of participants was overwhelmingly positive. They found it empowering and transforming. This is discussed further in Chapter Four. But how does this happen? What is going on here? How does ritual do what it does? These questions are addressed in the rest of this book by considering some of the insights and tools of ritual and cultural studies.

Ritual

The term 'ritual' has been used in a whole range of theories and disciplines in a variety of ways.[1] Although it would seem to be a simple task, defining ritual turns out to be much more complicated than at first it seems. Ritual is variously seen as maintaining the way things are, subverting the status quo, a performance, re-enacting myths, therapeutic, formal, changing, given, constructed, about words, about symbols, about experience, empty, enriching, sacred, secular, for individuals, for groups, for societies, a key to interpreting culture, the way a culture passes on its values, rigid, flexible, a

---

[1] For example Alexander, 1997, p.140 lists the following disciplines who have made the study of ritual more central: anthropology, sociology, comparative study of religion, religious studies, historical studies, social psychology, theatre studies and performance theory, and semiotics. He also stresses that the study of ritual has become more interdisciplinary

universal phenomenon, about particular rites, and about a particular way of acting.

It is clear that many of these represent contrasting views. A few definitions of ritual serve as a simple illustration of this range of perspectives. A dictionary of liturgy and worship describes ritual as 'the proscribed form of words which constitute an act of worship'.[2] This contrasts with 'Ritual is the symbolic use of bodily movement and gesture in a social situation to express and articulate meaning'.[3] Victor Turner states that 'ritual is part of society's communication code for transmitting messages to one another about matters of ultimate concern and about those entities believed to have enunciated, clarified and mediated a culture's bonding axioms to its present members.'[4] Another definition of his – perhaps the best known one – is 'prescribed formal behaviour for occasions not given over to technical routine, having reference to beliefs in mystical beings or powers regarded as the first and final causes of all effects'.[5] Others focus on religion as well, but emphasize the experiential encounter 'Ritual arises from and celebrates the encounter with the numinous or sacred.'[6] Some apply ritual to 'all culturally defined behaviour'.[7] A more recent definition typically focuses on performance 'Ritual defined in the most general and basic terms is a performance, planned or improvised, that effects a transition from everyday life to an

---

[2] In J.G. Davies 'A New Dictionary of Liturgy and Worship', 1986, under the entry 'ritual'
[3] Bocock, 1974, p.37
[4] Victor Turner from an article he wrote entitled, *Ritual, Tribal and Catholic* in 'Worship' (1976) 50(6), quoted in Harris, 1992
[5] Turner, 1982, p.79
[6] Zuesse, 1987, p.405
[7] Leach, 1968, p.524

alternative context within which the everyday is transformed'.[8]

Later, I attempt to outline the development of several theories of or approaches to ritual. This is designed to give an overview of a body of theory. Categorizations are a construction, a way of telling a story and the boundaries of categories blur, and some theorists fit into more than one category at different periods of their life.[9] In retrospect, it is often easy to see that theories are responses to the period they were written in. In this sense they are not neutral or objective, whatever the intentions of the author, but they are guided by a worldview[10] or paradigm. Thomas Kuhn's study in scientific theory[11] showed how theories are guided by worldviews or paradigms that assume that the universe is a particular way and that we can know about it in particular ways. Change from one era to another does not involve a simple evolution of scientific knowing but a paradigm shift, a 'revolution' in which the old paradigm loses credence and a new one takes its place. This sort of paradigm thinking has been applied in understanding the development of a range of disciplines. For example, Webber applies it to understanding the history of the church, which falls into six discernible paradigms or eras.[12] In each era, Christians struggled to incarnate the faith in that particular culture and a new paradigm emerged. In the change from one era to another, some people stay with the old paradigm and others adapt to the new one. So the story

---

[8] Alexander, 1997, p.139
[9] Victor Turner is one such example
[10] The term 'worldview' seems to be used in a variety of ways. I use it here as defined by Al Wolters, 'the comprehensive framework of ones beliefs about things' (Wolters, 1985, p.2)
[11] Kuhn, 1969
[12] Webber, 1999, p.13-17. Hans Kung and David Bosch pioneered this approach

of the development of theory is not a simple case of one theory ending and another replacing it. In the Church theologies, approaches to mission and the styles of church emerging from different eras all continue into the present in various ways. In the same way, the story of the development of theories about ritual isn't a case of one theory ending and another replacing it. Most of the approaches are still current or at least drawn upon in the present.

Later in this book, contemporary approaches are explored in more detail. It is helpful to see how these interplay with earlier theories, both drawing on some of their insights and deconstructing others.

Ritual and Religion

The notion of ritual first emerged as a formal term of analysis in the 19th-century. It was first used to identify and describe what was believed to be a universal category of human experience.[13] It emerged as part of a wider debate about the origins of religion, which was seeking to answer the question of whether religion and culture were rooted in myth or in ritual.[14]

Early theorists debated whether myth was 'mere error and folly' or a deliberate philosophical attempt to understand the world albeit with 'primitive reasoning'.[15] Others argued that myth was not as significant as ritual. Robertson Smith saw ritual as the primary component of religion serving 'the basic social function of creating and maintaining community'. He argued that 'the myth was derived

---

[13] Bell, 1992, p.14
[14] Bell, 1997, p.3
[15] Leading figures supporting this view were Andrew Lang 1844-1912, Edward Tylor 1832-1917

from the ritual and not the ritual from the myth'.[16] According to Bell, these early theorists' work led to the development of three powerful schools of interpretation of religion.[17]

1. The 'myth and ritual' school largely associated with James Frazer's famous work, *The Golden Bough*,[18] argued that to understand a myth you had to understand the ritual it first accompanied. The myth lived on after a ritual practice had ceased, so the ritual was the key to understanding the myth. They developed a single ritual pattern (the dramatization of the death and resurrection of the king as a god) that they saw as the key to unlocking the meaning of a lot of ancient cultural activities.

2. Phenomenologists of religion emphasized myth more than ritual, they resisted the reduction of religion to a primitive explanation stressing that religious experience was 'a real and irreducible phenomena',[19] and emphasized the ahistorical universal aspects of religious experience. This approach tended to minimize the importance of ritual. Mircea Eliade (1907-1986) was the leading figure, and he gave primacy to myths and symbols. In this school, ritual or rites are the re-enactments of the deeds performed by the gods and preserved in myths[20] – 'A major strategy employed by ritual is simply to re-enact with the participants' own bodies the primeval or constitutive acts by which the cosmos came into being'.[21]

---

[16] Robertson Smith, 1969, p.18
[17] Bell, 1997, p.5
[18] Frazer, 1911
[19] Rudolf Otto particularly explores this notion in, *The Idea of the Holy*
[20] Eliade, 1959
[21] Zuesse, 1987, p.410

3. The third approach was psychoanalytic; of which Freud was the key figure. The connection here with the earlier theorists is that Freud read and was influenced by them. He saw internal psychic conflict as arising from both repressed desires and taboo desires. Ritual was a way of trying to resolve these inner conflicts. He wryly observed that when these were carried out in a socially acceptable manner they 'are called poetry, religion and philosophy'.[22] Others have developed the psychoanalytic approach with a more positive slant on ritual, emphasizing its therapeutic value.

Ritual and Society

A new set of questions emerged about how ritual functions within society. In much the same way that theories about ritual and religion developed in response to a set of questions about ritual and myth, this new set of questions led to a new theoretical approach.

Not surprisingly in view of the questions, this approach was known as 'functionalist'. Emile Durkheim, in his *Elementary Forms of the Religious Life*, opened it up.[23] He was still studying religion but shifted the focus onto its social rather than psychological dimensions. For Durkheim religion was about 'normal social and natural life: the rainfall, the crops, good hunting, good health, children, and social continuity'.[24] Rituals were about regulated symbolic expressions of sentiments or values that hold society together. His focus on the social purposes of ritual developed into a general school among British anthropologists.[25]

---

[22] Freud in Introduction to Reik, 1975, p.10
[23] Durkheim, 1915
[24] Zuesse, 1987, p.412
[25] Bell, 1997, p.27

Leading social functionalists were, Radcliffe Brown and Malinowski. For them 'ritual was seen as a means to regulate and stabilize the life of the system, adjust its internal interactions, maintain its group ethos, and restore a state of harmony after any disturbance'.[26]

As well as the function of ritual, a further question began to emerge around the meaning of rituals. Van Gennep (not a functionalist himself) suggested that the meaning of a rite could only be understood in terms of how it is used in its original context/setting. In his book, *Rites of Passage*, like so many others, he is still trying to trace the universal patterns of ritual which he described in a three stage sequence: separation, transition and incorporation.[27] One of the results of his study was that it drew attention to the symbolism in the rituals and the meaning in them.

Victor Turner, a very influential figure, drew heavily on Van Gennep's work. He gradually became disenchanted with a view of ritual as social control. He developed the theory that life contained two styles of being in the world – structure and anti-structure. 'It is as though there are two major models for human interrelatedness, juxtaposed and alternating. The first is of society as a structured, differentiated and often-hierarchical system…The second is of society as an unstructured or rudimentarily structured and relatively undifferentiated communitas, community or even communion of equal individuals who submit together to the general authority of the ritual elders'.[28] Ritual could function to maintain structure or to subvert it. Turner was writing this in the sixties when

---

[26] Bell, 1997, p.29
[27] Van Gennep, 1960
[28] Turner, 1969, p.96

perhaps it is not surprising to discover scholars thinking of ritual as having subversive, creative and culturally critical capacities.

Another significant focus of Turner's work that was to become more of a focus for what ritual means was on symbolism. He drew out the complex nature of symbols and their multivalence, their ability to have 'many meanings, and each is capable of moving people at many psycho-biological levels simultaneously'.[29] His work is considered in more detail later in this book with regard to ritual and change.

Another key theorist at this time was Mary Douglas. She came at the same issues as Turner but from a different angle, drawing heavily on Durkheim. She recognized that the view of ritual as functioning to maintain society had led to ritual becoming 'a bad word signifying empty conformity'.[30] She was interested in what made a society have more or less ritual and argued that 'people at different historic periods are more or less sensitive to signs as such...the perception of symbols in general, as well as their interpretation is socially determined'.[31] She developed a scheme of 'group' and 'grid' (which parallel closely Turner's notions of communitas and structure) to show whether a society would have more or less ritual. Societies with strong group or grid will have more. However, some of her key insights relate to symbols. She showed that even anti-ritualists are merely adopting one set of symbols in place of another – for example fundamentalists reject the magic of the Eucharist but become magical in their attitude to

---

[29] Turner, 1969, p.129
[30] Douglas, 1970, p.19
[31] Douglas, 1970, p.28

the bible![32] She also highlighted the lessons to be learned for religious bodies 'to set their message in the natural system of symbols'.[33] She lamented the loss of a common set of symbols by the purging of old rituals, from which we arise 'ritually beggared' and without much weight of history.[34]

Ritual and Culture

The focus on questions surrounding meaning led to a new set of theories in ritual. Theorists who began to go beyond functionalism and structuralism were called symbolists and culturalists.[35] Rather than looking to the symbols in ritual to explain the structures of social organization, they treated them more like an independent system of cultural symbols, a language for communication. The question now was on 'what a symbol means within the context of the whole system of symbols within which it was embedded'.[36]

Levi Strauss used a linguistic model to explain cultural phenomena other than language. He argued that, '…if we want to understand art, religion, or law, and perhaps even cooking or the rules of politeness, we must imagine them as being codes formed by articulated signs, following the pattern of linguistic communication'.[37] He then proceeded to try and uncover the grammar-like rules that govern the production of cultural systems like ritual, particularly emphasizing binary oppositions. The notions of language and communication were developed by many others

---

[32] Douglas, 1970, p.40
[33] Douglas, 1970, p.200
[34] Douglas, 1970, p.41
[35] Bell, 1997, p.61
[36] Bell, 1997, p.61
[37] Levi Strauss, cited in Bell, 1997, p.62

and are still very current. Culture is frequently seen as an, 'ensemble of texts', which can be read and interpreted semiotically.[38] Rituals can be read in this way.

In *Cultural Studies*, Roland Barthes is perhaps the most influential figure in interpreting signs.[39] He uses the terms 'denotation' and 'connotation' to describe the primary and secondary levels of communication. It is at the secondary level that the notion of 'myth' is produced and made available for consumption. The move from denotation to connotation is only possible because of a shared cultural repertoire. Without this shared code, connotation would not be possible.[40] So for example, in the labyrinth, a candle with three wicks in the centre denotes light, but the connotation is the presence of God the Trinity in Holy Space.

In the seventies, theories of ritual as performance gained currency. Turner developed this notion in his later work. He saw ritual as dramatizing social conflict and resolving it in ritual. The idea of cultural performance is developed by Geertz, Tambiah and Schechner, and is used to stretch the boundaries of what is ritual into activities such as sport, theatre, play, political ceremonies, and concerts as they all share several basic qualities. Schechner draws a continuum with 'efficacy' (ability to effect transformation) at one end and 'entertainment' at the other. He argues that if the purpose of a performance is to entertain, then it is theatre. If it is to transform then it is ritual.[41] This notion of ritual as performance still

---

[38] Geertz is one such cultural anthropologist
[39] See Hall, 1997, p.30-41
[40] Storey, 1996, p.92
[41] Schechner cited in Bowie, 2000, p.159-160

seems to be the most popular in current work.[42] Catherine Bell is, to my knowledge, the only current theorist to raise questions about the implications of the use of performance as a metaphor for ritual.[43] She develops the notion of ritual as practice, which is discussed below.

Contemporary Emphases in Ritual Studies

We have traced the relationship various theorists have constructed between ritual and religious, social and cultural questions and concerns. In newer studies, it has been increasingly recognized that religion, society and culture are mutually influential. Here, I attempt to highlight some emphases in newer approaches to ritual. This is not an exhaustive list.

Not a Universal Phenomena

The attempt of earlier studies to find what universally defines ritual, to come up with a grand theory that explains it, has been rejected. 'Ritual is not a universal cross-cultural phenomenon but a particular way of looking at and organizing the world that tells us as much about the anthropologist and his or her frame of reference as the people or behaviour being studied'.[44] Because of the difficulties surrounding definitions of ritual, some have preferred to identify the 'family characteristics' of ritual, expecting only some to show up in specific instances.[45] Others have preferred to focus on

---

[42] See for example Alexander, 1997; Bowie, 2000; Grimes, 1990
[43] Bell, 1992, p.42-46
[44] Bowie, 2000, p.151
[45] Grimes, 1990, p.14

ritualisation, as a particular way of acting.[46] And many have just focused on a specific context being concerned with 'the native point of view'.

Dynamic not Rigid

Ritual was once conceived of as formal, traditional and unchanging with routine as its hallmark. Whilst it is still recognized that it can be these things, there is much greater emphasis on the dynamic nature of ritual and its capacity to be experimental, subversive, and counter-cultural. Rites can be invented, individual, new. Grimes describe the staggering diversity of counter-cultural ritualizing in America.[47]

Symbols not Words

Whereas earlier studies tended to give primacy to words, there is now much more emphasis on symbols and the cultural system of meaning within which they are embedded. The symbols used need to communicate by connecting with the cultural world of participants for ritual to be effective.

Embodied

There is a tendency to focus on ritual's 'experiential, performative, physical, bodily and gestural features'.[48] Bocock suggests that 'the use of the body, together with visual and aural symbols places ritual at the centre of attention if our concern is with the split in our culture between the body and the mind: the non-rational and the

---

[46] See for example Bell, discussed elsewhere in this book
[47] Grimes, 1990, p.121
[48] Alexander, 1997, p.142

over rational'.[49] Earlier theorists' analyses are criticized for emphasizing cognitive and verbal aspects to the virtual exclusion of emotions.[50] Part of the appeal of theories of performance is the heightened multi-sensory experiences they afford to the whole embodied person.

Transforming

Ritual has a role in transformation of society and individuals. Earlier theories posited a simple mirroring of society and culture, but it is now recognized that ritual is generative of society and culture. 'Ritual is constitutive of experience since it transforms the experiential base out of which people live their everyday lives'.[51] Transformation is discussed further below.

Fashionable

Presently, ritual is a fashionable idea. This is so both in the academic world but also in people's everyday lives. 'Ritual has become a counter-cultural fad, the object of rampant experientialism, that is the belief that experience *per se* is authoritative'.[52] In spite of a decline in interest in institutional forms of ritual 'the need for ritual and the practice of ritual have not declined, on the contrary they have intensified and increased as institutionalized forms have lost their appeal and effectiveness'.[53]

---

[49] Bocock, 1974, p.30
[50] Scheff, 1979, p.114
[51] Alexander, 1997, p.141
[52] Grimes, 1990, p.135
[53] Shorter, 1996, p.28

Open to the Sacred

Whilst institutional religion has declined, there has also been a resurgence of interest in spirituality. This is discussed further below. But ritual is seen by many as a 'window open on one side to the eternal'.[54] In many discussions 'spirituality' and 'the sacred' are fairly vague notions but there is nonetheless a hunger to encounter something divine whether by turning inwards or outwards. 'What is the experience of ritual after all? Is it not the act of entering into the presence of the Holy?'[55]

Ritualisation as Practice

Catherine Bell suggests that there is an underlying logic of sorts to most theoretical discourse on ritual and that this discourse is fundamentally organized around an opposition between thought and action in a variety of ways.[56] She suggests this is problematic. 'In the final analysis the results of such a differentiation between thought and action cannot be presumed to provide an adequate position *vis a vis* human activity as such. Naturally, as many others have argued before, the differentiation tends to distort not only the nature of so-called physical activities but the nature of mental ones as well.'[57] In its place she proposes an alternative way of thinking about ritual activity that stresses the primacy of the act itself and how its strategies are lodged in the very doing of the act itself. 'Ritualisation' is the term she uses to describe ritual as a strategic way of acting in specific social situations. Rather than focus on

---

[54] Shorter, 1996, p.121
[55] Shorter, 1996, p.110
[56] Bell, 1992, p.47
[57] Bell, 1992, p.48

ritual as a distinct, autonomous and universally recognizable set of activities or as an aspect of all human activity, she draws attention to the way in which ritual actions distinguish themselves in relation to other actions.

She draws from practice theory, in particular the work of Pierre Bourdieu. He uses the term 'habitus' to refer to 'the unconscious dispositions, the classificatory systems and taken for granted preferences'[58] which an individual has that operates at the level of everyday knowledge and are inscribed onto the individual's body i.e. they are part of who they are as persons. The insight that this gives is 'to confront the act itself' by addressing the 'socially informed body' with all its senses. The body is the factor that unifies all practice. Bourdieu writes that these senses include 'the traditional five senses...But also the sense of necessity, and the sense of duty, the sense of direction and the sense of reality, the sense of balance and the sense of beauty, common sense and the sense of the sacred, tactical sense and the sense of responsibility, business sense and the sense of propriety, the sense of humour and the sense of absurdity, moral sense and the sense of practicality, and so on'.[59] Bell adds that a 'sense of ritual' would be a vital addition to the list in most cultures.[60] Practice, then, is an irreducible term for human activity and Bell highlights four features of practice that are then used as a basis to discuss ritual activity. Practice is

    1) situational;

    2) strategic;

    3) embedded in a misrecognition of what it is in fact doing

---

[58] Bourdieu as discussed in Du Gay *et al*, 1997, p.97
[59] Bourdieu, 1977, p.124
[60] Bell, 1992, p.80

and

4) able to reconfigure a vision of the order of power in the world, or 'redemptive hegemony'.

First, to say that human activity is situational is to recognize that what is important to it cannot be grasped outside of its immediate context.

Second, to say that it is strategic is to suggest that it employs schemes and tactics to improvise and negotiate through everyday situations. De Certeau's classic *The Practice of Everyday Life*[61] focuses on the tactical[62] nature of everyday practices of consumers. He particular points out peoples many and varied ways of 'making do' that subvert the dominant systems in which they develop.

Third, by saying that it is involved in misrecognition of what it is in fact doing, Bell means that a practice does not see itself do what it does. There is invisibility. 'It sees what it intends to accomplish but it does not see the strategies it uses to produce what it does accomplish, a new situation'.[63] Redemptive hegemony is a synthesis of Burridge's notion of 'redemptive process' and Gramsci's notion of 'hegemony'.[64] Hegemony recognizes the system of power relations in a society. Redemptive process describes the way people can act within the system of power so that the power relations are reproduced and people have a sense of their place within them but they can still negotiate space to act within

---

[61] De Certeau, 1984
[62] Somewhat confusingly, De Certeau uses 'tactic' in the way Bell uses 'strategy'. He reserves the term 'strategy' for something very different
[63] Bell, 1992, p.87
[64] As cited in Bell, 1992, p.83

that in ways that are empowering for them.

So fourth, saying that practice is able to reconfigure a vision of the order of power within the world (redemptive hegemony) is to recognize that practice negotiates the existing power relations in such a way as to empower individuals within it, but without them either leaving or destroying the system. The St Paul's Labyrinth is now discussed using this notion of ritualisation as practice and the four features of practice.

Making Sense of St. Paul's Labyrinth

To begin to make sense of the St Paul's Labyrinth its context is important. This is the first aspect of practice. How does walking a labyrinth in St Paul's Cathedral in London in the year 2000 relate to the multitude of ways of acting in the culture?

Culture Shift

David Lyon uses the term 'Postmodern Times'[1] to describe the cultural context of life in the Western world. This is a helpful use of the term postmodern and I will use it in the same way. 'Postmodernism' tends to be associated with a philosophical revolution linked with the likes of Derrida, Lyotard, Baudrillard, Foucault and Rorty, but most people do not read their texts or enter

---
[1] Lyon, 2000

into the debate at this level. (This is not to say that these debates are not significant or important). But they do experience the social changes and cultural shifts taking place in their everyday world – in other words they live in postmodern times.

These times have changed radically from previous generations. 'Reality isn't what it used to be'.[2] There is widespread agreement on this much at least, though exactly what the contours of the new world look like is harder to say. We know where we have come from 'modernity' but we are not quite sure where we have arrived! 'Modernist sentiments may have been undermined, deconstructed, surpassed, or bypassed, but there is little certitude as to the coherence or meaning of the systems of thought that may have replaced them. Such uncertainty makes it particularly difficult to evaluate, interpret and explain the shift that everyone agrees has occurred'.[3] Hence the attachment of the 'post' to 'modern', rather than a completely new term. Some writers see us as living between times – 'we live between the ages when the previous culture of modernity still holds sway and power but the emerging culture is present with vigour'.[4] Others see that modernity is dead and buried and still others that the postmodern times are nothing more than 'the latest move on modernity's chessboard'.[5] However postmodern times are in some ways a reaction to modernity, so it helps to have some grasp on modernity.

---

[2] This is the title of a book by Walter Anderson, 1990
[3] Harvey, 1990, p.42
[4] Riddell, Pierson and Kirkpatrick, 2000, p.19
[5] Natoli, 1997, p.11

The Crisis of Modernity

Modernity is the term used to describe the worldview of the Enlightenment era. Its foundations were laid in the Renaissance whose thinkers had elevated humanity to the centre of reality.[6] Whilst modernity is characterized by rationality, objectivity, human autonomy, mastery of the world, universal knowledge and absolutes, the heart of the matter is that 'the spirit of modernity is the spirit of progress'.[7] Goudzwaard, in *Capitalism and Progress*, most succinctly expounds this. In this, he identifies the religious nature of modernity's faith in Progress as its grounding conviction. 'The theme of progress has penetrated Western society so profoundly because it was able to present itself as a faith in progress, as a religion of progress. This is also why the present day crisis of the idea of progress has the depth of a crisis of faith'.[8]

With the tools of science to give knowledge, technology to give power and mastery of the environment and with the goal of economic growth, human beings sought to build the promised land, a new world, the new Jerusalem. What was envisioned was 'a veritable utopia of prosperity and progress in which the whole human race would be united...Human progress is not only possible but inevitable if we allow autonomous human reason the freedom to investigate our world scientifically. By this free and open investigation we have confidently believed, humanity will be able to acquire the technological power necessary to control nature and bring about the ultimate goal: increased economic consumption and

---

[6] Grenz, 1996, p.60
[7] Middleton and Walsh, 1995, p.19
[8] Goudzwaard, 1979, p.248

affluence, with resulting peace, fulfilment and security.'[9]

This story no longer rings true. It sounds like a fairy tale, too good to be true. Walsh and Middleton use the metaphor of a building for the project of modernity with three floors of science, technology and economic growth, under girded by a foundation of human autonomy. The building is rotten from the foundation up and now, in the 21st-century, this is finally becoming manifest to its dwellers.[10] Put another way, 'The old certainties of the Enlightenment are no longer secure, and there is a widespread feeling that science and technology have ultimately failed to deliver the goods'.[11] Two world wars, the realization that much of the vision was built on African slavery, colonialism and imperialism, the environmental crisis, AIDS, escalating poverty, and the Vietnam war, are just some of the factors that have contributed to its demise. As one songwriter sung ironically 'we tried to build the New Jerusalem and ended up with New York ha ha ha!'[12] This is not to deny the many positive benefits of modernity, but to recognize the widespread loss of faith in its grounding convictions.

Postmodern Times

Postmodern times, then, come in the wake of this crisis of faith. It is impossible to make sense of them without realizing that this is so. What, then, are the contours of postmodern times pertinent to a discussion of religion to help us make sense of the St Paul's Labyrinth? It seems every author has their own take on what these

---

[9] Middleton and Walsh, 1995, p.19
[10] Middleton and Walsh, 1995, p.23
[11] Drane, 2000, p.7
[12] 'Laughter' by Bruce Cockburn on 'Waiting for a miracle', 1987, Revolver Records

contours are, and each one differs in some way. I am particularly focusing on ones that seem to relate to religion and contemporary culture.

Spirituality

The standard theory used to make sense of religion since the fifties has been secularization, that the Western world is in an advanced state of living without gods. Modern society runs on non-religious principles. It is inhospitable to faith, religion and the sacred. Church attendance and social influence declines and religion becomes increasingly marginal to society at large.[13] On the surface, this seems to be a tenable theory. Certainly in the UK, Christian churches, particularly the main denominations are only too painfully aware of their waning influence and the decline in church attendance over the last twenty years, especially amongst the young.[14]

However in recent years, much to the surprise it seems of some commentators, there has been an explosion of interest in spirituality. Drane observes that people are responding in two ways to the current cultural shift. The first is to immerse themselves in a hedonistic lifestyle and ignore questions of ultimate meaning. But 'many others are trying to deal with the threatened disintegration of our culture by engaging in a self conscious search for spiritual answers that will hold out the possibility of providing a secure basis on which to build new lives in the third millennium'.[15] But this is not doing anything to affect the decline in numbers attending

---

[13] Lyon, 2000, p.21
[14] See for example Brierley, 2000
[15] Drane, 2000, p.vii

churches. Institutions are suspect[16] and 'the great majority of these spiritual explorers do not make any connection between their personal quest and the existence of the church'.[17] Tom Beaudoin narrates his own story in *Virtual Faith* and I suspect it is typical of many when he writes, 'I was awash in popular culture and alienated from official religion. Despite all this I still considered myself unmistakably spiritual. By this I meant that I thought about religion, I thought there was more to life than materialism, and I pieced together a set of beliefs from whatever religious traditions I was exposed to at the time.'[18]

Why is it that so few people who are searching for spiritual meaning either look for it or find it in the institutional church? Several writers have concluded that the church has so wedded itself to the culture of modernity that it's the only frame of reference in which it knows how to operate. Cray suggests that, 'People young and old are looking for spiritual answers but the last place they expect to find them is in the Christian church. The institutional church is assumed to be part of the old (modern!) order that has failed'.[19] Going to church feels like visiting another era. This is seen in the cerebral nature of expressions of faith, emphasis on doctrines, propositional truth, the pervasive rationalism, and the old fashioned patriarchy of the British Empire that still seems so evident. Whilst elsewhere in the culture there is a fascination with mystery, the numinous, angels, heaven and the after-life, 'at best

---

[16] Beaudoin, 1998, identifies four characteristics of the spirituality of Generation X. Suspicion of institutions is one
[17] Riddell, 1998, p.11
[18] Beaudoin, 1998, p.14
[19] Cray, 1998, p.13

the church seems to speak uncomfortably about them'.[20]

Postmodern times are tactile, symbolic, and image based while in the church, the Word seems to have been imprisoned in words rather than becoming flesh. Those best touched by the intuitive, artistic and creative find little that speaks to them in church. Postmodern times elevate experience and community. Church is not the kind of place for expressing emotions like grief and failure. Grimes identifies ritual as a feature of postmodern times.[21] But the ritual on offer in churches somehow feels empty and boring. It's what Scheff calls 'overdistancing'[22] i.e. has an absence of any emotion. Postmodern times celebrate the body and being human. The dualism in much of the theology of the church has left a view of bodies and matter as bad and this in turn has been destructive of ritual. Because of this, when people do look to Christian rituals they, 'find ritual action which often contradicts their own basic feelings'.[23] This is all compounded by a general failure to take postmodern times and in particular peoples spiritual search seriously.

This new explosion of spirituality is easily dismissed as individualistic, and reflective of consumerist attitudes and lifestyles. It does not, at first, seem to detract from the secularization thesis either because these private beliefs do not impact the way society runs. But, as I argue below, consumption is the way society runs now, or at least a very significant factor. So then this is precisely

---

[20] Drane, 2000, p.97
[21] Grimes, 1990, p.24
[22] Scheff, 1979, p.120. Scheff argues that one of the functions of good ritual is to create appropriate distance for people to express emotions. 'Overdistancing' leaves no room for expressing emotions
[23] Bocock, 1974, p.38

where we should look to find openings for religious activity. They are just invisible to many institutional leaders and to academic accounts of the modern world.[24]

There is a story told by Australian Aboriginals of a mighty river that once flowed across the land.[25] Generations were sustained by its flow but gradually it ceased to flow. Some waited for its return but others went to see what had happened. It turned out that the river still flowed but had changed course upstream creating a billabong on the curve where the Aboriginals still sat. The river still flowed but elsewhere. Religious life in postmodern times has not dried up as predicted by the theorists, but it is being relocated. Patterns of religious behaviour are being restructured. The river is flowing elsewhere.

Consumption and CITs

One of the most significant features of postmodern times is that we live in a culture based on consumption. In modernity identity and social integration were found in production and the work place. Now 'consumption has become production',[26] and 'individual choice' has replaced progress as the core value and belief of our society'.[27] Baudrillard says that, 'consumption is a system of meaning like a language...commodities and objects, like words...constitute a global, arbitrary and coherent system of signs, a cultural system...a code with which our entire society

---

[24] Lyon, 2000, p.32, 24
[25] McGrath cited in Lyon, 2000, p.20
[26] Twitchell, 1999, p.286
[27] Cray, 1998, p.6

communicates and speaks to itself'.[28] This consumer culture is facilitated by the growth of communication and information technologies (CITs) and new media whose impact cannot be underestimated. Within this consumer culture social interaction and organization take on a new cultural pattern. People find and construct meaning routes through everyday life to help them negotiate the terrain. These are no longer simply defined by tradition, family or geography. The range of choices confronting people is immense. In part, they negotiate meaning in society via networks[29] and relationships and the construction of identity (or identities).[30] Both are related. Identity is increasingly seen as something constructed via taste and selective consumption, and is used to make distinctions from others.[31]

The networks of relationships are often those from whom approval is sought through similar lifestyle and tastes. There is a sense in which this can lead to a 'symbolic membership' of a group or network.[32] The flows of information round these networks are increasing aided by the CITs and the whole process seems to be very fluid and changing. Usually they have some location in place but not necessarily and certainly not exclusively. Culture is increasingly fragmented and there are a range of worldviews, meanings, lifestyles and subcultures at play. Culture is in this sense

---

[28] Baudrillard cited in Du Gay *et al*, 1997, p.91
[29] Castells, 1996
[30] Bauman, 1995, p.81 suggests that the key issue in postmodern identity construction is 'avoidance of fixation' or keeping the options open, hence the use of 'identities'
[31] Sarah Thornton discusses this in relation to club culture and the way taste and selective consumption are used by clubbers to define themselves over and against the mainstream (Thornton, 1995)
[32] Bauman, 1992, p.50

a 'site for contested meanings'[33] within which people find manifold ways of 'making do', of living 'the practice everyday life'.[34]

The implications for religious practice are enormous. Lyon suggests that within a consumer culture, religion is best viewed as a dynamic cultural resource rather than an organizational form or fixed entity.[35] This is a neat move and it certainly seems to be the way a lot of individuals and groups treat it, though I suspect it would be one resisted by the guardians of declining religious institutions.

Tourists and Pilgrims

St Paul's Cathedral has in the region of 5000 visitors a day. These largely fall into two categories: tourists and pilgrims. Some tourists arrive in coach loads and have a guided tour of the cathedral, others are on their own or in small groups, going round at their own pace. The week of the labyrinth in March coincided (intentionally) with the beginning of the season of Lent. In amongst the tourists there were clearly a good number of pilgrims, especially on Ash Wednesday, when many had come for the service to be marked with ash on their forehead.

Zygmunt Bauman is wonderfully evocative and perceptive in his descriptions of peoples 'life strategies' in postmodern times. His analysis of the times (as concluded above) is that consumption has taken centre stage and become 'the integrative bond of society'.[36] One of the themes he returns to time and again is the

---

[33] Storey, 1996, p.26
[34] De Certeau, 1984
[35] Lyon, 2000, p.141
[36] Bauman, 1992, p.49

construction of identity. He contrasts modern and postmodern approaches to identity concluding 'the hub of postmodern life strategy is not identity building but the avoidance of being fixed'.[37] He sees the pilgrim as an appropriate allegory for identity building under the conditions of modernity. The pilgrim knows where he or she is going and weaves each event or site of pilgrimage into a coherent 'sense-making story' and is living with a purpose of fulfillment.[38] The tourist (along with the stroller, vagabond, and player)[39] is the most appropriate metaphor to describe postmodern life strategy as avoiding being fixed. 'The tourist is the epitome of such avoidance. Indeed tourists worth their salt are the masters of the supreme art of melting the solids and unfixing the fixed. First of all they perform the feat of not belonging to the place they might be visiting; theirs is the miracle of being in and out of place at the same time.'[40] The tourist is a systematic seeker of new and different experiences, but needs to keep moving, traveling light. Relationships with locals are likely to be skin deep and must not tie the tourist down. They must be able to get up and move on and shake off the experience whenever they wish.

Some of the considerations of 'situation' then for the St Paul's labyrinth are that it is in postmodern times in a time of increased hunger for spirituality but decline in institutional religion. Situated in a time when consumption has moved to centre stage, it is visited both by pilgrims who will be looking to make some meaningful connection with the ritual and their life story and

---

[37] Bauman, 1995, p.89
[38] Bauman, 1995, p.87
[39] Bauman, 1995, p.91
[40] Bauman, 1997, p.89

tourists who will have the experience and attempt to move on. Both may be treating it (and religion) as a cultural resource to weave into the meaning routes they construct through the postmodern maze. This is 'strategic', the next aspect of practice.

Strategic – Alternative Worship, Popular Culture & Tricksters
Some of the strategies employed in the labyrinth are considered in this section. Alternative worship is an inculturation of the Christian faith in postmodern times. Ritual, popular culture, 'wholespeak', and the resources of the Christian tradition are used to negotiate change and imagine new worlds. A comparison is made with the roles of prophets, artists and tricksters.

Inculturation
Contextualization, incarnational mission and inculturation have all become buzzwords in mission studies. Inculturation is 'the totality of a religion integrating with the totality of a culture'.[41] There has been an increased recognition that the history of mission has been something of a mixed blessing.[42] Often the sharing of the gospel overseas was wrapped up with the sharing of Western culture. Whilst there are inspiring stories of missionaries who took the task of contextualization seriously and introduced many people to the risen Christ communicated in the language and symbols of their culture, there are equally stories of the gospel being shared hand in hand with an imperialism whose legacy still lives on today.

---

[41] Atta-Bafoe and Tovey in their essay, 'What does inculturation mean?' in Holeton (editor), 1990, p.14

[42] See Bosch, 1991 for a comprehensive discussion of the history of mission

Hopefully, churches and mission agencies today have learned the lessons from the past. The Anglican Communion has certainly considered these issues both in relation to mission and to worship and liturgy. The 1988 Lambeth Bishops conference passed two resolutions as follows:[43]

1. Christ and Culture

This conference a) recognises that culture is the context in which people find their identity; b) affirms that...the gospel challenges some aspects of the culture while endorsing others; c) urges the church everywhere to work at expressing the unchanging gospel of Christ in words, actions, names, customs, liturgies which communicate relevantly in each society.

2. Liturgical Freedom

This conference resolves that each Province should be free...to seek that expression of worship which is appropriate to the Christian people in their cultural context.

Beginning from these two resolutions, the *York Statement* was then prepared for the whole Anglican Communion on liturgical inculturation. The following are some quotes from the statement:

'Liturgy to serve the church should be truly inculturated.'

'Just as language forms change from one place or time to another, so the whole cultural appropriateness of styles and expressions of worship should be ready to vary similarly.'

'Inculturation must therefore affect the whole ethos of corporate worship, not only the texts but also for example, the use of

---

[43] These are recorded in the *York Statement* in Holeton, 1990, p.8

buildings, furnishings, art, music, and ceremonial.'

'True inculturation...implies a willingness in worship to listen to culture...it has to make contact with the deep feelings of people. It can only be achieved through an openness to innovation and experimentation, an encouragement of local creativity, and a readiness to reflect critically at every stage of the process, a process which in principle is never ending.'

'We long to see...well equipped imaginative liturgists.'

'Our lack of inculturation has fostered both the alienation of some Christians and an over ready willingness of others to live in two different cultures, one of their religion and the other of their everyday life. Other Christians again have left our churches because of this cultural insensitivity. Similarly non-Christians have found the foreignness of the church a great barrier to faith.'[44]

I quote from it at length because it is so insightful. The encouragement for innovation and creativity, the need for connection with peoples feelings, the scope of change required, and the awareness of the way the church has alienated people by its lack of inculturation is astonishing to read in such an official document. These insights were written to help the Anglican churches round the world develop their own authentic expressions of faith. But if the analysis outlined above is correct and the forms of institutional church life in the UK are wedded to modernity, the same insights need to be applied on our own doorstep to inculturate the faith in postmodern times. Sadly, there is very little evidence that the Anglican Church is aware of this or doing anything about it. Riddell recognizes the problem when he writes, 'Inculturation, people

---

[44] The *York Statement* is written in full in Holeton, 1990, p.8-11

movements, development, syncretism, contextualization; these have all become familiar subjects of theological investigation in relation to foreign mission. Unfortunately, few of the resulting insights have made much impact on home base. The one massive gap in the church's expertise is how to do mission in the post Christian West'.[45] According to Bosch, the Enlightenment paradigm has heavily influenced missionary endeavors in the West.[46] In the process the gospel has largely been reduced to a rational and didactic event. One of the many consequences of this is that the church has become 'blind to ritual'. Karecki argues that ritual desperately needs to be re-discovered as a key to wholeness in mission.

Alternative Worship

Alternative worship groups in London developed the St Paul's labyrinth. Alternative worship is a strategic Christian response to postmodern times, an attempt to inculturate the gospel – 'Alternative worship arises from the need for the church to engage with a culture shift from the patterns of life which took shape in modernity to a faith which brings the authentic message of Christ to bear on life in postmodernity'.[47] The description of inculturation outlined above in the York Statement could almost be read as a rationale for it.

The Drapers list the following as characteristics of alternative worship (nearly all of which are features of the labyrinth):

---

[45] Riddell, 1998, p.12
[46] Bosch, 1991, p.343
[47] Roberts, 1999, p.3

A renewed exploration of creativity

A concept of faith as journey

Less rigid or hierarchical leadership structures

A holistic understanding of worship – our lives as worship

Affirmation of personal identity

An emphasis on relationships and community

A care for the environment and an exploration of our place within it

Risks taken, unusual things tried

Congregational involvement – interaction encouraged

An embrace of uncertainty

A focus on contemplation and meditation

A search for the transcendent and a sense of mystery and wonder

An emphasis on small locally based groups not big events

Cultural relevance not technology for its own sake

Use of symbolism that connects with people at different levels

A combination of ancient and contemporary

A commitment to change instead of self-preservation

Use of elements that both sides of the brain respond to – i.e. experientially and intellectually.[48]

    A glance through these characteristics immediately helps gain a good feel for the strategies employed and in particular how they contrast with some of the strategies employed by other Christian groups, tribes or denominations. Alternative worship is both a strategy for those involved to help them develop an expression of faith that is 'authentic' for them and it is also a strategy for mission and evangelism. Along with many other aspects of the church's life, evangelism is an area that feels stuck in

---

[48] In Grace e-zine/newsletter January 1998

another era. Many Christian denominations and organizations recognize that the old ways of doing evangelism no longer seem to work. For example Youth For Christ, in their strategy for 2000 identified as a priority what they termed 'reinventing evangelism'. A whole approach based on apologetics, persuading people of the truth of Christianity's claims is no longer answering the questions people are asking. In a culture swamped with advertising, people have had enough sales pitches. Those who claim to know all the answers are viewed with suspicion. Alternative worship does not go in for the hard sell. It is more under girded by a belief that if those developing worship find themselves at home in it then it will relate to their peers.[49] Its starting points are recognizing that many people are spiritually searching and looking for experiences to meet their hunger, but that they do not want to be dictated to by those who have already 'arrived'.

Success in evangelism has often been measured in terms of numbers responding and then joining a congregation/church. On this measure of success, alternative worship has been relatively unsuccessful. Groups have tended to remain small. Numbers becoming committed members of core groups are in their ones and twos. However, it is also typical of groups to have a stream of individuals and groups visiting their services sporadically. Many groups have done some soul searching on this issue. Why is it that what feels like them a great hope for the future of the church remains so small? In part, it may well be because groups have stuck with a congregational model of church which does not connect with peoples' meaning routes through a consumer culture and they are

---

[49] Dawn, 1997, p.49

measuring success in terms of that model. Most groups meet monthly or fortnightly. Whilst the style of worship relates to the emerging culture, the structure does not seem to in the same way. The challenge for alternative worship groups' inculturation lies here. What are the meaning routes, networks and flows of relationships in postmodern times? How might the Gospel relate to them?

The labyrinth offers a good example of a different (or complementary) approach. Its closest parallel is an art installation that directly appeals to the way tourists and pilgrims negotiate their way through life. Viewed and treated as a cultural resource, they can ignore it or choose to explore and experience it, weaving it into their own lives as they see fit. It is not in a Sunday service slot. It is on the track of tourists. There is no expectation or pressure on them to sign up or come back. It's offered as a gift. In a consumer culture, the availability of the CD to purchase in the cathedral shop means that they can relive the experience at home. The availability of connection via the Internet can enable further contact and conversation for those keen to pursue it. It may be that one or two tourists are so transformed by it that they will seek out a group to join. In this respect, the structure is more akin to an art collective than a congregation offering its art/worship as a cultural resource. In an art collective, the vast majority of people encountering the art are visitors. There is an inner core of members who give to, support and shape the vision of the collective. But these are a minority. Some combination of developing a core group of artists/worshippers who develop services, spaces for spiritual encounter, and products that are able to be used as a cultural resource by tourists in postmodern times alongside some way of developing the networks of relationships within which those same tourists relate is a challenge facing alternative worship groups.[50]

Alternative worship is not the only strategic Christian response available. The rise in fundamentalism in the world is seen by some as a strategic response because it offers certainties for those unable to live with the anxiety which comes from the tendency to keep options open at all times, to avoid fixation of identity.[51] The 'growth from below' of Pentecostalism around the world, especially in Latin America, is another.[52] In the recent survey of church attendance in England, evangelicalism is one area where small growth can be seen.[53] This is an area of the church that has been quick to develop strong tribal identities and to develop products in the marketplace, one response to a consumer culture. In charismatic evangelical churches, the experiential nature of worship and perhaps a contextualization of worship as rock concert or performance has been another strategic response. The Alpha course developed and franchised by Holy Trinity Brompton is another. Orthodoxy, perhaps particularly because of its iconic tradition has also experienced growth, although again the overall numbers in the UK are relatively small.

If, as has been argued above, religion is being treated as a cultural resource, there are also many individuals and groups whose strategies remain invisible as they are outside the observable institutions, whether they gather in pubs, homes, visit a variety of

---

[50] Thanks to Pete Ward who highlighted the issue of the appropriateness of the congregational model in conversations with the author
[51] Bauman, 1997, p.184
[52] Lyon, 2000, p.34
[53] Brierley, 2000, p.156

churches without becoming members of any, or meet in cyberspace or develop loose intentional communities to do a combination of all the above and more.

Ritual and Change

One characteristic that I would add to the above list of characteristics of alternative worship is the strategic use of ritual itself. Most alternative worship services or events incorporate some sort of ritual or symbolic act. In Grace's booklet on getting started in worship, they describe ritual as facilitating encounter with the divine. 'Again and again we find that God meets us in ritual so we nearly always try and incorporate some sort of ritual that everybody is involved it...it opens up a window in the soul and the community through which the breeze of the Spirit can blow. It seems to draw a service together and seal what has taken place. It helps move worship from the head to the heart'.[54] How ritual helps facilitate this encounter and empowers participants is considered further below. The question considered here is how the labyrinth as an example of an alternative worship ritual is strategic in relationship to change and its positioning within the wider church.

Victor Turner's notion of ritual as both structure and anti-structure was outlined above. Rather than ritual just being seen as maintaining social control, Turner introduced the notion that ritual as anti-structure could be subversive of structure and the status quo. Using Van Gennep's three phases of rites of passage as separation, margin (or limen) and aggregation, Turner particularly drew

---

[54] Grace booklet, *Fresh Vital Worship*, CPO, 2000

attention to the second 'liminal' or threshold period.[55] In this liminal phase of ritual, people slip through the network of classifications that normally locate positions in cultural space, they are 'betwixt and between'. It is particularly in this state that people are enabled to experience themselves and their world from a new point of view. Further, 'communitas' develops – 'for me communitas develops where structure is not'.[56] Turner explains that his choice of 'communitas' rather than 'community' is because community implies geographical location[57] (I suspect this is no longer the case). Communitas is spontaneous, immediate, and concrete relationships and community.

Those concerned with maintaining structure find these liminal situations dangerous or polluting, precisely because those in them do not fit the categories of structure. Different cultures have a whole range of phenomena parallel with liminality (he cites the court jester as one example).[58] 'Prophets and artists tend to be liminal and marginal people, 'edgemen' who strive with a passionate sincerity to rid themselves of the clichés associated with status incumbency and role playing and to enter into vital relations (communitas) with other men in fact or imagination'.[59] For society to function there has to be some form of dialectic between structure and anti-structure. In discussing Turner's work, Harris suggests that 'the subversive element in ritual has largely moved to art, music and theatre'[60] and that 'we must attend to the artists in our society if

---

[55] Turner, 1969, p.95
[56] Turner, 1969, p.126
[57] Turner, 1969, p.125-126
[58] Turner, 1969, p.125
[59] Turner, 1969, p.128
[60] Harris, 1992, p.54

we are to pick up criticisms of structure that need to be made'.[61]

The art critic and historian, Lewis Hyde, comes at the notion of liminal people from a very different angle. In his book, *Trickster makes this world*,[62] he discusses the trickster character in various mythologies – for example Coyote in North America, Hermes in Greece, Eshu in West Africa and compares them with more recent creators in the art world. He says this about Trickster: 'All tricksters are on the road. They are the lords of in-between. A trickster does not live near the hearth; he does not live in the halls of justice, the soldiers tent, the shaman's hut, the monastery. He passes through each of these when there is a moment of silence and enlivens each with mischief, but he is not their guiding spirit. He is the spirit of the doorway leading out and of the crossroad at the edge of town. He is the spirit of the road at dusk, the one that runs from one town to another and belongs to neither…In short, trickster is a boundary crosser. Every group has its sense of in and out, and trickster is always there, at the gates of the city and the gates of life.'[63]

There is a paradox in the trickster myth. For cultures to adapt and change and last, there needs to be space for the trickster whose function is to uncover and disrupt the very things the culture is based on - 'Social life can depend on treating antisocial characters as part of the sacred'.[64] Trickster needs a relationship to the powers that be, institutions and traditions that can manage to insist their boundaries be respected whilst at the same time

---

[61] Harris, 1992, p.55
[62] Hyde, 1998
[63] Hyde, 1998, p.6-7
[64] Hyde, 1998, p.9

recognizing that 'in the long run their liveliness depends on having those boundaries regularly disturbed'.[65] This is another way of saying that there needs to be a dialectic between structure and anti-structure. The role of the trickster turns out to be nothing less than opening the way to possible new worlds, as established categories of truth and property are disturbed via his cunning.

Hyde explores the way some contemporary artists take on the role of the trickster in society. We can also recognize very clearly the relationship in the Old Testament between the Prophets and the Kings, with the prophets playing the trickster role. It could be argued that Jesus is a trickster character, disturbing categories of who is in and out and imagining new worlds.[66] There is certainly a tradition of breaking with or reinventing tradition.

Ritual and the Effect of Tradition

It is commonly assumed that ritual is used to maintain a rigid and dogmatic tradition (i.e. as structure). Anti-ritualists arise precisely because of this view. As outlined above, Douglas explores the way in which the anti-ritualists then invent their own new rituals, even if they do not recognize them as such. She suggests that in the history of revolt and anti-ritualism then giving way to a new recognition of the need to ritualize, 'something is lost from the original cosmic ordering of symbols. We arise from the purging of old rituals simpler and poorer…the new sect goes back as far as the primitive church, as far as the first Pentecost, or as far as the flood, but the

---

[65] Hyde, 1998, p.13
[66] Harris, 1992, argues that anti-structure is more central to Christianity than structure, based on the life of Jesus read as anti-structure

historical continuity is traced by a thin line. Only a narrow range of historical experience is recognised as antecedent to the present state...There is a squeamish selection of ancestors: just as revolutionaries may evict kings and queens from the pages of history, anti-ritualists have rejected the list of saints and popes and tried to start again without any load of history'.[67] This is a useful insight and we can see this process at work in new religious movements in history with their take on the truth, which turns out to be very selective in the way Douglas describes.

However, this is not the only way to understand ritual and tradition. In postmodern times, when so little seems fixed and everything is in flux, tradition and continuity offer a sense of weight of history, an anchor point. The Christian tradition has 2000 years of history building on its previous 4000 years or so of history before that shared with the Jews. It is a tradition with a huge global network, diversity, examples and stories of ways in which the church has passed on the dangerous memory of Jesus, a catalogue of mistakes made and recovered from and a wealth of spiritual resources. But far from it being unchanging and fixed with a static set of 'cosmic symbols', it has been and is a living tradition. There are symbols (e.g. bread and wine) that have been passed down for thousands of years, but there are equally a whole range of new symbols and reinterpreted old symbols like the labyrinth. The kind of use of tradition to claim that things must remain the same is in that sense not faithful to tradition at all; it is rather a dead traditionalism.[68] The tradition has to be struggled with and reformed in order to be carried forward.

---

[67] Douglas, 1970, p.41
[68] Pelikan, 1984, p.65

To keep reforming religious tradition in a prophetic spirit is to be faithful.[69] One of the interesting things about the reformation of the Christian tradition is that while there are clearly limits to remaining faithful and legitimately staying within the tradition, it is from within the tradition itself that the tools and resources come to liberate from the way tradition has been used to oppress.[70] So the resources from within the tradition itself subvert the injustices and inadequacies of a religious tradition paradoxically.

Alternative worship groups are traditional in precisely this sense. Unlike the anti-ritualists Douglas describes who ignore the weight of history, this is precisely where they look to find the resources to reinvigorate the tradition, to make it live within postmodern times. Beaudoin suggests that Xers[71] 'must continually return to the resources of their inherited or freely chosen traditions, bringing them into the light of their own experiences of living in culture. They must take on their traditions, interpreting them anew for their unique culture'.[72] Ronald Grimes, who has pioneered Ritual Criticism, identifies three liabilities with new and invented rites:

a) *spiritual consumerism* – the consumer consumes rite after rite without ever being satisfied

b) *cultural imperialism* – the appropriation of sacred resources of other cultures and

c) *experimentalism* – always going for something new and

---

[69] Beaudoin, 1998, p.153
[70] Gadamer cited in Beaudoin, 1998, p.152
[71] A term used to describe 'Generation X', the characteristics of whom parallel those involved in alternative worship in many ways
[72] Beaudoin, 1998, p.153

lacking the courage to ever commit or make choices.[73]

The location of alternative worship within a tradition minimizes these liabilities. In this situation, it is clear that not 'anything goes'. But rather than there being rigid and fixed categories of what is right, however, the notion of 'faithful improvisation'[74] is a helpful way of making sense of how the reframing of tradition will be judged to be authoritative or not.

Within tradition, the use of ritual can be 'a particularly effective means of mediating tradition and change, that is as a medium for appropriating some changes while maintaining a sense of cultural continuity'.[75] One of the reasons for this is because ritual, even if relatively new and invented, has the semblance of having been passed down from previous generations. So the appropriation of ritual by alternative worship groups is highly strategic in this sense. An example of this is in the celebration of the Eucharist. Grace has developed several Eucharistic prayers that in the ritual are used in much the same way as one of the officially sanctioned prayers. The theological take of one is on the theme of hospitality, stressing Christ's open invitation to outsiders to share his table. If this was in a sermon, it could be thought of as someone's opinion, but in the heart of the Eucharist it seems to carry much more power and weight. It is in fact a highly subversive text, raising questions about the church's practice of excluding certain groups of people from sharing the bread and wine. But as a ritual form, it is a very effective medium for change, whilst maintaining a sense of continuity. 'Whether it is being performed

---

[73] Grimes, 1990, p.123-125
[74] This notion is developed by N.T. Wright, 1992, p.140-143
[75] Bell, 1997, p.251

for the first time or the thousandth, the circumstance of being put in the ritual form gives something the effect of tradition'187.[76]

The strategies of the St Paul's Labyrinth with regard to ritual and change weave together the threads discussed above. It is clearly a construct, an invented ritual. But it relates to a tool, a resource, an ancient spiritual practice within the Christian tradition, located in cathedrals, which has then been uniquely improvised with (hopefully in a faithful way).

Because of its appeal to the ancient tradition of labyrinth walking (explicitly stated on the users guide), it has the semblance of being passed down from previous generations. In reality we have very little sense of whether its use in practice, the theological takes of the meditations, and the symbolism involved is anything like that employed by Christians in the medieval cathedrals! We certainly know that the use of technology was not. Whilst Artress goes to great lengths to explain how the Chartres labyrinth design is an 'archetype',[77] a divine imprint somehow etched into the fabric of creation itself which gives it its energy, this seems equally in its own way to be a construct of its time, then reinvented and given its own meaning by contemporary users.[78]

Alternative worship lives on the margins, the threshold, of institutional religion. In this respect, I suggest that its role is akin to the trickster and prophet, continually crossing boundaries and

---

[76] Sally Moore and Barbara Myerhoff, cited in Bell, 1992, p.123
[77] Artress, 1995, p.3, p.150-153
[78] Three examples (of many) of the ways Artress constructs meaning for the labyrinth is by relating it to the mystical threefold path (Artress, 1995, p.28), by seeing at as tool for rediscovering the feminine principle and integrating it with the masculine (*ibid* p.157-165), and as a tool for therapeutic healing or enabling the psyche to meet the soul (ibid p.147)

moving boundaries, disturbing notions of truth and property, and doing nothing less than opening the way to new possible worlds. It is more anti-structure than structure. Communitas is developed *en route* between its members rather than an organized structure. Taking the labyrinth as an example, all sorts of boundaries are crossed and property shifted. Contemporary cultural artifacts – televisions, computers, Discmans, are where they should not be. What sounds at first like secular or 'new age' music is played behind meditations. All the rituals and symbolic acts are done without a priest in one of the most important cathedrals of the Church of England. In Holy Space, there is bread and wine that the participants can help themselves to just innocently sat there. It is not Eucharistic, or at least it has not been consecrated, but its symbolism is not lost on participants. All the words, images and rituals are invented by people who are not licensed, not 'experts'. Nothing has had approval from the liturgical committees. The artists have crept back into the church. Bodies, symbols, experience, the senses are involved in worship and prayer. Everyday language and items, rather than sacred, are used.

Where is the boundary now between sacred and profane? In this kind of shifting of boundaries, the labyrinth constructs a new world. But in doing so, those developing it claim to be being faithful to the tradition they are located in (albeit on the margins). Whilst many in positions of power in the institution view alternative worship as dangerous and a threat, the tradition needs to create spaces for the trickster to maintain its vitality.

There needs to be dialectic between structure and anti-structure.

Use of Popular Culture and the Everyday

'Matter out of place' is the title of one of the chapters in *Trickster Makes This World*.[79] In it, Hyde discusses the significance of dirt in many of the trickster myths. He draws on the work of Mary Douglas who describes dirt as matter out of place.[80] Any system orders the world in such a way as to designate some things that don't fit into the order as dirt – 'Dirt is the by-product of a systematic ordering and classification of matter, in so far as ordering involves rejecting inappropriate elements'.[81] So, for example, shoes are not dirty in themselves, but they are on the dining table, and food is not dirty but it is on clothing. Hyde suggests that 'if dirt is a by-product of the creation of order then a fight about dirt is a fight about how we have shaped our world'.[82] This is why trickster is always playing with dirt.

When the Sony Walkman first appeared it disturbed the boundaries between private and public worlds. It was 'out of place' in the symbolic ordering, or classificatory system of things. 'It offended people's ideas about what sort of activities belonged where'.[83] The meaning of the Sony Walkman in this respect was not something essential to the Walkman itself but 'a product of how that object is socially constructed through classification, language and representation'.[84] And further its meaning was in relation to other objects within the classificatory system and how it was different. Now today, the Walkman is much more an accepted part

---

[79] Hyde, 1998, p.173
[80] Douglas, 1966
[81] Douglas, 1966, p.36
[82] Hyde, 1998, p.198
[83] Du Gay *et al*, 1997, p.115
[84] Du Gay *et al*, 1997, p.115

of everyday life, and perhaps the panic has moved on to other new technologies like the Internet or mobile phone. The strategic use of popular culture and the everyday in the labyrinth is matter out of place, particularly because of its location in St Paul's. The prevalent view of culture in church still seems to be a high/low distinction. It has reified cultural forms located in the past. Putting on a Discman to listen to music that you would most likely hear in a club in the early hours of the morning is transgressing boundaries. It is not what you expect in a cathedral. In a consumer culture, people use the cultural resources available to them to make meaning (see above).

For large numbers of people, the resources of popular culture are what they use to construct identity and position themselves in relation to others, to develop some notion of authenticity. One use made of popular music in this way is to mark out space - 'forms of popular music and their stylistic innovations are one of the key ways in which local spaces can be appropriated and made habitable'.[85] So the use of the type of music in the labyrinth on Discmans is in this way a very strategic marking out of habitable space.

At the tenth station 'others', the walker is greeted with a laptop computer with a screen of virtual candles. In the meditation they are encouraged to 'light' a candle by clicking on the wick with the mouse and then to pray for someone. The candles are from the Internet site www.embody.co.uk designed for an 'online' spiritual experience of prayer. The choice to use virtual candles rather than real ones is strategic. The surprising thing is that, rather than being

---

[85] Bennett, 2000, p.69

naff, they do evoke a sense of sacred space, and the ritual seems to work with the technology, at least for a large proportion of participants. They function somewhat like an, 'icon of the present',[86] representing the mystery of the faith in the language of the here and now. The use of popular culture, indeed the whole approach to inculturation, is under girded by a theology of the incarnation - 'The incarnation gives us the model of relevance. God shows up on our turf speaking our language so that we might understand'.[87] The CDs of music and meditation were available for sale in the cathedral shop. Participants can thus reproduce the experience of the candles and pray at home on their own computer. In this way the ritual connects back into the everyday.

Narrowspeak vs Wholespeak

Theology is 'talk about God'. In this respect the St Paul's labyrinth is theological, it has plenty to say about God. The meditations are written out in full in the Appendix at the end of this book and it is immediately clear that Creation, The Trinity, the Incarnation, Relationships, Journey, Redemption, Transcendence and Immanence, Encountering God, Being Transformed are some of the significant themes. In many ways there is nothing unorthodox or surprising here. What is significant, I think, as a strategy, is the manner in which the labyrinth and meditations talk about God. 'We live in an age when our capacity for speech is vastly reduced'.[88] Les

---

[86] *Icons of the Present* is the title of a book by Edward Robinson in which he argues that to be faithful to tradition iconography needs to be earthed in the present to avoid the dangers of nostalgia and otherworldliness. (Robinson, 1993, p.29)
[87] Riddell, Pierson and Kirkpatrick, 2000, p.126
[88] Matthews, 2000, p.53

Murray contrasts the terms 'narrowspeak' and 'wholespeak' to elucidate his thinking on ways of talking about God.[89] He suggests that in recent times (modernity) God talk has been severely reduced to narrowspeak, the voice of reason, rational and didactic ways of talking, the discourse of prose. It is a language that has to make sense, be explained, and that everybody can understand. Wholespeak in contrast is a poetic discourse, mystical speech, a language that is 'truly dreamed'. This is very similar to Walter Brueggemann's appeal to the church to rediscover poetry rather than prose.[90] Both argue that the church needs to rediscover wholespeak or poetry, rather than feeling obliged to adopt the language of modernity. We might call this the 're-enchantment of speech',[91] speech that is in the language of the imagination, that recognizes the importance of symbols, images, myth, metaphors, music, the arts. 'Creative imagination, rather than some supposedly objective, rationally specifiable procedure that lies outside the domain of personal knowledge, is the key to knowing reality.

The truth is contained in symbols and the symbols are materially embodied. That is, it seems to me, a corollary of the incarnational and sacramental character of Christianity'.[92] This may be overstating the case. It is highly probable that speech about God in prose resonated in modernity, it was an appropriate contextualization and in any contextualization you gain some things

---

[89] *Embodiment and Incarnation* was the title of the 1986 Aquinas lecture given by Murray which contained these themes. It is cited in Matthews, 2000, p.53-55
[90] See especially in *Finally Comes the Poet*, where the introduction is called 'Poetry in a prose flattened world' (Brueggemann, 1989)
[91] Matthews, 2000, p.59
[92] Avis, 1999, p.8

and lose others. I suspect this is equally the case with 'wholespeak'. Nonetheless, it does succinctly capture the strategic way of talking about God employed in the labyrinth. Both the words of the meditations and the whole experience are full of imagination, artistic endeavor, in images, symbols and metaphors that are evocative of the Holy, but always suggesting that our speech is an inadequate vehicle for describing or capturing the Otherness of God.

The significance of the arts, the parallel between the labyrinth and an art installation perhaps lies here. This speech is intuitive to those producing the labyrinth, but it is also a language that resonates with many of the spiritual seekers in postmodern times. 'Whereas a large section of the contemporary church appears to be increasingly content with the pre-packed truths of a certain type of Christian exposition, the modern secular imagination, when it turns to religion, is more willing to linger with the different dimensions to religious awareness afforded by things like candles, icons, silence, Gregorian chants and hints of mysticism'.[93]

Misrecognition

The third aspect of practice that Bell describes is that it is involved in misrecognition of what it is in fact doing. By this she means that ritual is apt to misrecognise the relationship between its ends and its means in ways that promote its efficacy. She says 'It tends to see itself as the natural or appropriate thing to do in the circumstances. Ritualisation does not see how it actively creates place, force, event , and tradition, how it redefines or generates the circumstances to

---

[93] Matthews, 2000, p.22

which it is responding'.[94] Bourdieu (who influences Bell's notion of practice) articulates this blindness - 'it is because subjects do not know, strictly speaking, what they are doing, that what they do has more meaning than they realise'.[95]

This notion of practice seems to me to be patronizing. Indeed for alternative worship, it could be argued that one of its strategies is self-awareness about its own role in constructing both a ritual space and experience and how that will impact participants.[96] There is a sense in which participants in the labyrinth were caught by surprise. Some were moved to tears, issues in their lives addressed, others encountered the presence of God when they didn't believe in God (!). A participant described (enthusiastically) the labyrinth as 'sneaky'[97] because people just walked the labyrinth and before they knew it they were being surprised by this sense of encounter with God. But rather than this being about misrecognition, I think both tourists and pilgrims, 'sensation gatherers' as Bauman calls them, doing the labyrinth hope for an experience in this way. It is part of what they expect. So on this third aspect of practice I part company with Bell and agree with De Certeau in his dismissal of it in Bourdieu's work 'With these 'strategies'…knowledgeable but unknown, the most traditionalist ethnology returns…Today an ethnologist would no longer dare to say that. How can Bourdieu compromise himself thus in the name of sociology?'[98]

---

[94] Bell, 1992, p.109
[95] Bourdieu cited in De Certeau, 1984, p.56
[96] Roberts, 1999, p.17
[97] In conversation with the author after walking the labyrinth
[98] De Certeau, 1984, p.56

Redemptive Hegemony

The strategies and situation of the St Paul's labyrinth are closely related to the notion of redemptive hegemony. The relationship of alternative worship to the arrangement of power in the church and the way in which groups manage to carve out space to empower them and maintain resistant and subversive identities whilst still remaining within the system has been discussed above at length. This is one aspect of redemptive hegemony. The aspect discussed here is how the participant in the St Paul's labyrinth is personally empowered.

Transformation

The goal of ritualization is 'the creation of a ritualized agent, an actor with a form of ritual mastery, who embodies flexible sets of cultural schemes and can deploy them effectively in multiple situations so as to restructure those situations in practical ways'.[99] This is Bell's masterful description of how ritual does what it does. To get away from traditional notions of ritual, she develops a new way of talking about it that takes some getting used to.

To walk the labyrinth is to enter ritual space or a ritual environment. One of the most significant aspects of it is that the whole person, the ritual body, interacts with this environment. There is circularity to this interaction. It is both generative of it and moulded by it in turn.[100] So the simple act of dropping a stone in water to let go of pressures and concerns at the 'letting go' station say, does not merely communicate the need to let go. It produces a person freed from pressure in and through the act itself. Or the act

---

[99] Bell, 1997, p.81
[100] Bell, 1992, p.99

of walking slowly round the labyrinth with God rather than the usual rushing alone in urban life doesn't merely communicate the need to slow down, it is generative of a slowed down person aware of God's presence in life. It is in this sense that the labyrinth walker is a 'ritualized agent'. Many of the symbolic acts, as well as drawing on the Christian tradition, also draw from the insights of therapy in transforming persons.

Ritual mastery is the way in which schemes deployed in the labyrinth can then be used in a variety of circumstances beyond the rite itself. In the 'self' station the walker stops to hear some verses affirming their uniqueness from Psalm 139 as they look in a mirror. The next time they look in a mirror, they may well see themselves in a new way.

The connection with ordinary everyday things in the labyrinth is particularly strategic in this sense. One walker who had a fear of heights somehow had enough confidence having walked the labyrinth to then climb up to the whispering gallery in St Paul's directly afterwards – their fear was dispelled in the ritual.[101] One priest on duty in St Paul's who walked the labyrinth described the lingering impression of the 'noise' station and how he had been reflecting on it since.[102] He had deployed this scheme of the labyrinth back into the circumstances of his life. Ritual mastery then is 'an internalisation of schemes with which they are capable of reinterpreting reality in such a way as to afford perceptions and experiences of a redemptive hegemonic order'.[103] This can be very empowering for participants. Many described it using the words a

---

[101] This account was narrated to the author in conversation
[102] Recounted in conversation with the author
[103] Bell, 1992, p.141

'powerful experience'.[104] Bell clearly accepts that ritual transforms persons and succinctly explains how it does so. Alternative worship groups have also discovered this for themselves. Bell seems to subscribe this transforming effect to the process of ritualisation itself. The alternative worship groups and planners of the labyrinth, as well as recognizing the power of ritualisation, see the transforming effect as more than a constructed experience. Their conviction is that the transformation is also affected by the Spirit of God whose presence is real, even though the Sacred always comes 'cloaked in cultural forms'[105] (in this case ritual/the labyrinth).

The powerful transforming effect of walking the labyrinth then does no less than produce new persons, enabled to see the world and act in it in a new way.

Consent and Resistance

The accusation could be made (and has been made) that those constructing ritual are being manipulative. However for this to be so it assumes that the walkers are easily duped. This is far from the case. In cultural studies, much recent work has focused on how meaning resides as much if not more with users and audiences rather than producers.[106] Meaning is located in the interchange between reader and text and the negotiated readings that result. Similarly ritualisation involves a mix of consent (at least enough consent to walk the labyrinth in the first place) and resistance from

---

[104] The information to support this is gleaned form conversations and from entries in the visitor's book at the end of the labyrinth where participants are invited to write their comments, thoughts or prayers.
[105] Beaudoin, 1998, p.156
[106] See for example Taylor and Willis, 1999

participants.

There are many ways in which participants resisted aspects of the labyrinth, whether skipping parts, disagreeing with them, or repeating parts several times. Because of the multivalence of symbols they were also able to create various levels of meaning relating to their own situations. Ritualized practices thus 'do not function as an instrument of heavy handed social control. Ritual symbols and meanings are too indeterminate and their schemes too flexible to lend themselves to any simple process of instilling fixed ideas'.[107]

---

[107] Bell, 1992, p.221

Concluding Remarks

The St Paul's labyrinth is an example of ritualization as strategic practice in postmodern times. The times are characterized by an increased hunger for spirituality and decline in institutional religion. Consumption and communication and information technologies (CITs) shape the way 'tourists' and 'pilgrims' treat religion as a cultural resource to weave into the meaning routes they construct to negotiate their way through life. The labyrinth offered as a resource in this way is a strategic part of alternative worship groups' approach to inculturating the Gospel. The use of ritual is an effective means for negotiating change both within the church tradition and its power relations and for the transformation of individuals who walk the labyrinth. Just as the trickster crosses boundaries, disturbing notions of truth and property, the labyrinth's blend of ancient, contemporary and the everyday opens the possibility of new worlds in the heart of the Christian tradition. The labyrinth in this respect is a prophetic sign of hope for Christian spiritual practice in postmodern times.

Appendix:
Labyrinth Meditations

1: Inward Journey

You are on a journey, a journey towards the light that is God.

A journey towards the centre of the labyrinth. And out again.

A journey towards God. And out again.

A journey of receiving...and then giving.

Walk with expectancy.

As you journey, reflect on what you see, hear, think. Expect to discover the wonderful, the fantastic.

Open your eyes wide, use your senses - this is no senseless journey.

Breathe deeply. Relax. Don't rush; savour the moment.

Be aware of others - we are travelling together. And focus on moving Godwards.

As you move towards the centre of the labyrinth confess and let go of things that hinder your relationship with God.

Shed images or projections of yourself so that you can be real with God.

Let go of what other people think you should be, their expectations of you, their projections.

As you journey unmask yourself, peel away the layers - grow by subtraction.

Prepare your inner self - the you of you - to meet with God.

At the beginning of time the earth was in darkness; and we are in darkness.

But we shall move towards the warmth and nourishment that is God, our life source.

God spoke the word, and the Word was God. And there was light.

God created and created and keeps on creating. God sees that it is good.

God labours to bring life; and gives birth to abundance. It is good.

In the beginning was the Word, and the Word was with God, and the Word was God. The Word was with God in the beginning. Through the Word all things were made; without the Word nothing was made that has been made. In the Word was life and that life was the light of men and women. The light shines in the darkness but the darkness has not understood it.

The Word became flesh and blood and moved into the neighbourhood...

Full of grace and truth...

The world that was in darkness has seen a great light - heralded by a birth-star in the dark night sky in Bethlehem. Just as the wise men journeyed onwards towards God by following the star, so we ask you to journey, to press on toward the light of life.

Our task is seldom easy; after all, we see through a glass dimly. But we have seen - maybe just glimpsed - the light, and tonight we travel towards the centre of the labyrinth as a symbol that we are going after the light of God.

As a seed grows towards the light, allow yourself to do the same. Trust the Creator God with your whole self. Acknowledge who you are, and who you are becoming. Show your amazing colours. Stand tall.

On a journey, we sometimes find ourselves on the open road; plain cruising.

Sometimes we have to navigate terrible junctions. Sometimes we are held up.

Sometimes the road is wide and clear. And sometimes it narrows, almost frighteningly. Sometimes our travelling companions are keeping up with us.

Sometimes they have gone on ahead and left us. Sometimes it is they who lag behind.

Who are your travelling companions? How much do you value them? What are you like to travel with? When the road gets rough and steep...will you be there to support your friends, your family, those you worship with?

Have you stopped to see how far you have come, recently? Have you encouraged each other to press on? As you journey through the labyrinth, resolve to encourage those you travel with in faith and life.

And remember the beautiful, strange paradox of our faith. We search after God, we travel towards God, as pilgrims. And yet God, too, is with us. As a guide. And as a traveller. God hasn't promised an easy ride, but has promised to sustain us.

God is faithful, God will not desert you.

God is the pulse of the cosmos, God will not let you die.

God is love. They will comfort you.

Three in One, One, but not the same...

...as we are one, but not the same.

Connected, but individual. Apart, but together. A part of each other.

As you journey, begin to focus on God.

God is at the centre of the universe, as the Sun is at the centre of our solar system.

The source of all warmth and love and light and life.

God pours out into the universe with life-giving light, with love.

Experience the love, feel the warmth. Choose life.

Can you receive from God? You may not like accepting and receiving hospitality. Yet God, our host, has so much to offer us and give us: all the riches of a relationship.

Jesus himself was a guest at a wedding in Cana – we've heard it all before.

He turned the water into wine. (It's our proof-text against puritans.) Vintage stuff.

Jesus was a guest - of humanity. The heavenly host, who laid on a harvest of abundance for the world, the creator, my provider, became the guest of the animals in the stable, the villagers of Nazareth, the religious leaders in the Temple, the prostitutes, drunkards, tax collectors. He let us play host, did away with the VIP pass, ate, drank, and was probably merry. Became one of us, dined at our table. Ate the same bread, drank the same wine - everybody having a good time. Shared stories; shared our story.

When he left the table, he left bread and wine.

He, himself, left; but he left himself. The guest, once more, became the consummate Host.

Through all the interference and the static of on-screen culture, God's voice is breaking through the airwaves:

'Are you receiving me? Are you receiving me?'

2: Noise

Sound engineers speak of two things - signal and noise.

The signal is the meaningful part of a transmission.

The noise is all the unwanted stuff that interferes with our ability to hear and understand the signal.

Our lives are full of noise - so much information, so many messages, all competing for our attention.

We find it hard to find the signal.

Take some time to identify the noises around you one by one:

traffic; children playing; dogs barking; the hubbub of life...

As you recognise each one, savour it and then place it to one side.

What are the noises on the inside?

that song you can't get out of your head; thoughts that won't stop chattering; nagging worries; hurt; anger; things you have to do tomorrow...

Identify them one by one, listen to them and place them to one side.

Let God still the oscilloscope of your soul,

turn the noise off

and give you peace.

Then listen for his signal.

Be still

quiet

listen

still

be

3: Letting Go

Take some slow deep breaths and relax.

Begin to let go of the tensions in your body.

Feel the pressure and busyness slipping away.

As you draw breath think of how your body is using oxygen. It is being carried to every part of your body. Feel the life it brings. As you exhale, you breathe out carbon dioxide which you don't need. Trees and plants take this in. They then produce oxygen which sustains you.

You are an integral part of God's mysterious and wonderful creation.

In front of you is a pile of stones and a pool of water.

Take a stone from the pile.

Imagine that all your concerns and worries are held in the stone.

Hold the stone tightly and name the concerns and worries in your mind.

Hold the stone over the pool of water.

In your own time let it go.

Watch your concerns and worries fall.

Imagine them falling into God's lap.

How does it feel to release them?

4: Hurts

The world is broken in many ways - our relationships with others, God, the planet and ourselves.

What hurtful things have been said to you?

What hurtful things have been done to you?

If you were to write a word or draw a symbol to describe this what would it be?

You might like to draw it now

What hurtful things have you said?

What hurtful things have you done?

If you were to write a word or draw a symbol to describe them what would it be?

You might like to draw it now

Look at your symbols.

Do you want to take them with you? Or do you want to let them go?

'If we confess our sins God is faithful and just and will purify us from all unrighteousness'

Jesus said if you let go of the hurtful things people do to you, so God will also let go of the hurtful things you do. This is forgiveness.

Think carefully. Are you willing to 'let go'?

If you are then throw the symbols in the bin.

Let go of them as God lets go of the hurtful things you do.

You are loved. You are free. You are forgiven

5: Distractions

In front of you is a map

In the centre is a compass

The needle of the compass points directly north.

Also on the map are some small magnets, some 'false norths'.

Try moving these magnets around the compass. See what happens

The 'false norths' pull the needle away from true north.

If God is true north, what are the false norths distracting your focus away from God?

As you identify these false norths move them to the edge of the map.

Refocus on true north...

Begin to focus on God

6: Holy Space

This is holy space

God is here - you are welcome

This is your space to be with God

And God's space to be with you

Make yourself at home

Be yourself

Be real

There's no rush

Let God love you

Let God know you

Let God heal you

Let God speak to you

Receive from God

Commune with God

Feed on God

7: Outward Journey

As you journey out of the labyrinth take your encounter with God with you.

Reflect on how this encounter might affect or change you.

John says that God became flesh and blood and moved into the neighbourhood -

think about how you might allow God to be made flesh in your life and in your neighbourhood.

Freely, freely you have received. Freely, freely give...

Take: eat. Take: out.

As we meet with God and receive, think about taking the light out into the world.

And about what it might illuminate.

Even if you are only a bright spark, kindle.

Kindle the life and the light you received from the heart of the Son.

You might even get fired up. You might blaze a trail,

stand up for others, seek out injustice,

protest on behalf of the innocent, carry a torch for the unloved, demonstrate for love.

Demonstrate love itself.

Mary was also given a challenge. She was asked to carry The Word, the pulse of the cosmos within her. She literally carried God into the world.

Mary said yes and changed the course of history -

took a gamble on the divine, flouted the odds,

evened the score with darkness,

carried the light of the world and allowed it to shine.

So that we might see it, and respond.

She had a choice, as we have a choice.

Choice cuts: sometimes like a sword to the heart. It did for her.

Choose carefully.

Jesus was no robot - he made agonising choices.

Stood up, stood out and was crucified for it.

Look where that got him, they said. It got him all the way to us.

You can choose a lifestyle. Or you can choose life. The choice, as they say, is yours.

So where do we go from here? As the journey seems to be ending, it is only just beginning. We are caught between a world that is passing, and a world that is yet to come. A world of the now, and the not yet...

Someone once spoke of a road less travelled. Of a narrow path.

Today, we are going on a journey...

8: Self

'You created my inmost being

You knit me together in my mother's womb

I praise you because I am fearfully and wonderfully made

Your works are wonderful, I know that full well'

When you look in the mirror what do you see?

Do you like the psalmist see someone that is 'fearfully and wonderfully made'?

Does what you see make you want to praise or cringe?

What do you think Jesus meant when he said to love others as we love ourselves?

What is the you of you?

Stop to feel your pulse. Life is running through you. Life is a gift of God

Feel your fingertips. Look at the pattern on them. Each is unique

You are unique

You are made in God's image

You are loved by the Creator who is proud of you, the created.

Look again at the mirror

Ask God to show you the real you, the you without image, the you that God sees

9: The Planet

You are out in space

Floating, weightless, calm and secure

Seeing things clearer than ever before

Watching the earth

Listening to its uninterrupted stream of noise

From the silence of infinite space

From here there are no visible countries

It's not like a map or a globe

There are no lines for territories

No colours to mark out countries, historical separations, human definitions....

Just rock, sea, forest and desert

Evolving, eroding, reforming, colliding

Life, death, birth, turning -

Movements and currents

Massive and caught up in the energy of creation

You are looking for signs of ownership but none are visible

You are looking for clues of permanence

But all is slowly changing

To who does this all belong?

Who has the right to claim its power, plunder its resources?

You are out in space

Breathless and patient

Awe-struck and motionless in front of this big, blue, bright ball

This great glittering, god-filled gift

This unbounded blessing you can only call

Home

In the palm of your hand you hold a small seed

This seed contains all the information needed to reproduce its own kind

You plant the seed in some soil

As you do so, feel the moist earthiness of the soil

Think of the darkness the seed experiences before it can spring to life -

on the brink of creation there is darkness

As you plant the seed you are participating in one of the greatest mysteries of the cosmos -

you are co-creating with God. Together you give birth to life.

As the seed grows and flowers it is a symbol of your love and care of nature, creation, of the planet, of home.

10: Others

Reflect on the web of relationships within which you live

Who are the other people with whom your life is connected?

One of the oldest ways of praying we know is lighting a candle.

Light a candle and pray for one or more of the people

Give thanks for them

Hold them in prayer before God

11: Impression

In front of you is some sand

You remove your socks and shoes

Tread in the sand to leave your footprints

Step back and look at them

Where you have walked has left an impression

What will be left of us when we've left,

when we're gone under down into darkness, the earth and memory? When our dust and ashes have shaken themselves down and reverted to their original state will their miraculous interlude have leaned on history's rudder?

What will be left of us when we've left?

What traces will we leave?

Will the evidence be compelling?

What will the surviving witnesses say?

How will they know we were here?

Will the future be better because of what we did with our present?

How many breaths make a life?

How long does it take to make a difference? (When can I start?)

What will history say of us when we're history too?

What will be left of us when we've left?

Bibliography

Alexander, Bobby C. (1997) **Ritual and Current Studies of Ritual: Overview** in Glazier, Stephen D., editor (1997) **Anthropology of Religion: A Handbook** Wesport, Connecticut: Praeger

Artress, Dr Lauren (1995) **Walking a Sacred Path: Rediscovering the Labyrinth as a Spiritual Tool** New York: Riverhead books

Avis, Paul (1999) **God and the Creative Imagination: Metaphor, Symbol, and Myth in Religion and Theology** London and New York: Routledge

Bauman, Zygmunt (1997) **Postmodernity and its Discontents** Cambridge: Polity Press

Bauman, Zygmunt (1995) **Life in Fragments** Oxford: Blackwell

--- (1992) **Intimations of Postmodernity** London: Routledge

Beaudoin, Tom (1998) **Virtual Faith: The Irreverent Spiritual**

Quest of Generation X San Fransisco: Jossey Bass

Bell, Catherine (1992) **Ritual Theory Ritual Practice** New York: Oxford University Press

Bell, Catherine (1997) **Ritual: Perspectives and Dimensions** New York: Oxford University Press

Bennett, Andy (2000) **Popular Music and Youth Culture** Basingstoke: Macmillan press Ltd

Bocock, Robert (1974) **Ritual in Industrial Society** London: George Allen and Unwin Ltd

Bourdieu, Pierre (1977) **Outline of a Theory of Practice** Trans. by Richard Nice Cambridge: Cambridge University Press

Bosch, David (1991) **Transforming Mission** New York: Orbis Books

Bowie, Fiona (2000) **The Anthropology of Religion** Oxford: Blackwell

Brierley, Peter (2000) **The Tide is Running Out** Christian Research

Brueggemann, Walter (1993) **The Bible and Postmodern Imagination** London: SCM Press

--- (1989) **Finally Comes the Poet** Minneapolis: Fortress Press

Castells, Manuel (1996) **The Rise of the Network Society** Oxford: Blackwell

Cowan, Painton (1979) **Rose Windows** London: Chronicle, Thames and Hudson

Corbett, Peter (1998) **Pathfinders: Walking Medieval Labyrinths in a Modern World** Published on the Grace Cathedral web site at http://www.gracecathedral.org/enrichment/features/fea_19981120_txt.shtml

Cray, Graham (1998) **Postmodern Culture and Youth**

Discipleship Cambridge: Grove Books Ltd

Davies, J.G., editor (1986) **A New Dictionary of Liturgy and Worship** London: SCM Press Ltd

Dawn, Maggi (1997) **You Have to Change to Stay the Same** in Cray et al (1997) **The Post Evangelical Debate** London: Triangle

De Certeau, Michel (1984) **The Practice of Everyday Life** California: University of California Press

Deedes, C.N. (1935) **The Labyrinth** in Hooke, S.H. (1935) **The Labyrinth: Further Studies in the Relation Between Myth and Ritual in the Ancient World** London: SPCK

Douglas, Mary (1970) **Natural Symbols: Explorations in Cosmology** Barrie and Jenkins

Douglas, Mary (1966) **Purity and Danger** London: Routledge

Drane, John (2000) **Cultural Change and Biblical Faith** Carlisle: Paternoster

Du Gay, Paul; Stuart Hall, Linda Janes, Hugh Mackay, Keith Negus (1997) **Doing Cultural Studies: The Story of the Sony Walkman** London: Sage

Durkheim, Emile (1965) **The Elementary forms of the Religious Life (1915)** trans

J.W.Swain New York: Free Press

Eliade, Mircea (1959) **The Sacred and the Profane** New York: Harcourt Brace Jovanovich

Fairchild, Kristen (1997) **The Labyrinth: A Medieval Tool for the Postmodern Age** Published on the Grace Cathedral web site at http://www.gracecathedral.org/libraries/discontinued/textures/labyrinth.shtml

Favier, Jean (1988) **The World of Chartres** New York: Abrams

Frazer, James George (1911) **The Golden Bough 3rd edition 10 vols (1955)** London: Macmillan

Freitas, Lima De **Labyrinth** in Eliade, Mircea, editor (1987) **The Encyclopedia of Religion volume 8** New York: Macmillan Publishing Company

Geoffrion, Jill (1999) **Praying the Labyrinth** Cleveland, Ohio: The Pilgrim Press

Glazier, Stephen D., editor (1997) **Anthropology of Religion: A Handbook** Westport, Connecticut: Praeger

Goudzwaard, Bob (1979) **Capitalism and Progress** Toronto: Wedge and Grand Rapids, Michigan: Eerdmans

Grenz, S J (1996) **A Primer on Postmodernism** Grand Rapids, Michigan: Eerdmans

Grimes, Ronald (1990) **Ritual Criticism: Case Studies in its Practice, Essays on its Theory** Columbia: University of South Carolina Press

Hall, Stuart, editor (1997) **Representation: Cultural Representations and Signifying Practices** Sage Publications

Harris, Chris (1992) **Creating Relevant Rituals** E.J.Dwyer

Harvey, David (1990) **The Condition of Postmodernity** Oxford: Blackwell

Holeton, David R. editor (1990) **Liturgical Inculturation in the Anglican Communion** Nottingham: Grove Books Ltd

Hyde, Lewis (1998) **Trickster Makes This World** New York: North Point Press

Karecki, Madge (2000) **Religious Ritual as a Key to Wholeness in Mission** published in **Missionalia: the Journal of the Southern African Missiological Society** on the internet at http://www.geocities.com/Athens/Parthenon/8409/missalia.htm

Kern, H. (1982) **Labyrinthe** Munich: Prestel

Kuhn, Thomas (1969) **The Structure of Scientific Revolutions** University of Chicago Press

Lawlor, Robert (1982) **Sacred Geometry, Philosophy and Practice** New York: Thames and Hudson

Leach, Edmund (1968) **Ritual** in Sills, David, editor (1968) **International Encyclopedia of the Social Sciences volume 13** New York

Lyon, David (2000) **Jesus in Disneyland: Religion in Postmodern Times** Cambridge: Polity Press

Matthews, Melvyn (2000) **Both Alike to Thee: The Retrieval of the Mystical Way** London: SPCK

Middleton, Richard and Walsh, Brian (1995) **Truth is Stranger Than it Used to Be: Biblical Faith in a Postmodern Age** London: SPCK

Natoli, Joseph (1997) **A Primer to Postmodernity** Oxford: Blackwell

Otto, Rudolf (1917) **The Idea of The Holy (rev ed 1929)** New York: Oxford University Press

Pelikan, Jaroslav (1984) **The Vindication of Tradition** Yale University Press

Reik, Theodor (1975) **Ritual: Pyscho-analytic Studies** Westport, Connecticut: Greenwood Publishers

Riddell, Michael (1998) **Threshold of the Future: Reforming the Church in the Post-Christian West** London: SPCK

Riddell, Pierson and Kirkpatrick (2000) **The Prodigal Project: Journey into the Emerging Church** London: SPCK

Roberts, Paul (1999) **Alternative Worship in the Church of England** Cambridge: Grove Books Ltd

Robertson Smith, William (1969) **Lectures on the Religion of the Semites (1889)** New York: KTAV Publishing House

Robinson, Edward (1993) **Icons of the Present** London: SCM Press Ltd

Saward, Jeff (1999) **Ancient Labyrinths of the World (3rd ed)** Thundersley, England: Caerdroia

Scheff, T.J. (1979) **Catharsis in Healing, Ritual and Drama** University of California Press

Shorter, Bani (1996) **Susceptible to the Sacred: Psychological Experience of Ritual** London: Routledge

Storey, John (1996) **Cultural studies and the Study of Popular Culture: Theories and Methods** Edinburgh University Press

Taylor, Lisa and Willis, Andrew (1999) **Media Studies: Texts, Institutions and Audiences** Oxford: Blackwell

Thornton, Sarah (1995) **Club Cultures** Cambridge: Polity Press

Turner, Victor (1969) **The Ritual Process: Structure and Anti Structure** London: Routledge

Turner, Victor (1982) **From Ritual to Theater and Back** New York: PAJ Publications

Twitchell, James B, (1999) **Lead Us Into Temptation: The Triumph of American Materialism** Columbia University Press

Van Gennep, Arnold (1960) **The Rites of Passage** London: Routledge and Kegan

Webber, Robert (1999) **Ancient Future Faith** Grand Rapids, Michigan: Baker Books

Wolters, Al (1985) **Creation Regained** Leicester: IVP

Wright, N.T. (1992) **The New Testament and the People of God** London: SPCK

Zuesse, Evan M. (1987) **Ritual** in Eliade, Mircea, editor (1987) **The Encyclopedia of Religion volume 12** New York: Macmillan Publishing Company

Printed in the United Kingdom
by Lightning Source UK Ltd.
123435UK00001B/186/A